Germany 1918–45

RICHARD RADWAY

Contents

Hodder & Stoughton

A MEMBER OF THE HODDER HEADLINE GROUP

From the Second Reich to the Weimar Republic

Why did the Second Reich come to an end in 1918? What sort of republic was set up in 1919?

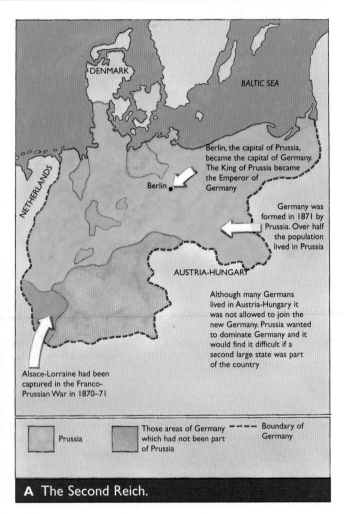

Berlin, the capital of Prussia, became the capital of Germany. The King of Prussia became the Emperor of Germany

Germany was formed in 1871 by Prussia. Over half the population lived in Prussia

Although many Germans lived in Austria-Hungary it was not allowed to join the new Germany. Prussia wanted to dominate Germany and it would find it difficult if a second large state was part of the country

Alsace-Lorraine had been captured in the Franco-Prussian War in 1870–71

Prussia	Those areas of Germany which had not been part of Prussia	– – – Boundary of Germany

A The Second Reich.

What was the Second Reich?

Germany was a new country. It had only come into existence in 1871. Before this date the area of Central Europe where German-speaking people lived was made up of a number of states. In 1870–1 the largest of these states, Prussia, had defeated France in a war. After this victory Prussia organised the other states into an empire, known as the Second Reich. *Reich* is the German word for empire. Hundreds of years before there had been a German-dominated empire in Central Europe. This had been known as the 'Holy Roman Empire' and so was regarded as the First Reich.

The Second Reich did not contain every German who lived in Europe. Prussia wanted to control the new Germany and so the other large German state, Austria, was not allowed to join. It remained part of the Austro-Hungarian Empire. Many of those Germans who did not live in the Second Reich dreamed of a time when a Greater Germany would be created, that is a Germany containing all the lands where Germans lived.

Kaiser Wilhelm

The Second Reich was ruled by an emperor known as the Kaiser. He was an **hereditary** ruler. He had enormous power. He could choose and sack ministers. He also controlled foreign policy and could declare war. In 1888 the 29-year-old Wilhelm II became Kaiser. He was a great nephew of Queen Victoria of Great Britain. In 1888 Britain was the world's most powerful country. As the world's first industrial country it dominated world trade. It also had an empire which ruled a quarter of all the people in the world. Wilhelm was determined to create a Germany which was as great as Britain. As source B shows, German industry was built up so that Germany overtook Britain as the world's leading trading nation.

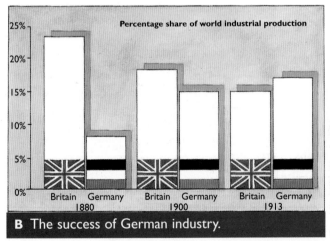

Percentage share of world industrial production

B The success of German industry.

Areas of Africa were conquered to create a German overseas empire. Britain had a huge navy to protect her empire and trading interests.

Queen Victoria gave Mount Kilimanjaro, the highest mountain in Africa, to Kaiser Wilhelm as a birthday present.

Wilhelm ordered the creation of a similar navy for Germany. Britain felt threatened and built more and even bigger ships. An arms race had begun.

The First World War

War broke out in 1914. Germany believed that they would win a quick victory. Things did not go according to plan. Unlike 1871, this time Paris did not fall to the invading German army. Both sides dug themselves into trench lines which stretched from the English Channel to the mountains of Switzerland. Trenches were difficult to attack and so the war settled into a stalemate. Neither side was strong enough to defeat the other. For the soldiers four years of hell had begun. Millions of men died. Those who survived lived in the appalling squalor of the trenches, never knowing when they too would die or suffer terrible injuries.

German defeat

Four years of stalemate finally ended in November 1918. The British naval blockade of German ports meant that Germany was running short of food and vital war supplies, such as rubber and oil. Perhaps even more significant was the decision of America to enter the war. This meant that Britain and France suddenly found their armies reinforced by new supplies of men and weapons, at a time when Germany was running out of both. General Ludendorff, the German commander, understood this problem. In March 1918 he launched Operation Michael. This was a desperate attempt to win the war before large numbers of American troops arrived. At first it was very successful, pushing the British back to the river Marne. But the very speed of the German attack took it too far ahead of its artillery, so that the German troops had little defence when British and Americans counter-attacked in August. Ludendorff realised that defeat was staring Germany in the face. He told the Kaiser that the war must be ended. In October the Germans asked the American President, Woodrow Wilson, to organise an end to the fighting. He agreed, but first demanded that the Kaiser must go. As starvation spread through Germany there were riots in many cities. On 30 October the German navy refused to launch a desperate attack on the British navy. The Kaiser finally agreed to **abdicate** and on 11 November an **armistice** was signed in a railway carriage at Compiègne, to the north of Paris. The war was over – and so was the Second Reich.

C Lance Corporal Adolf Hitler describes his experience of the war in a letter to a friend in February 1915:

Again and again one of our shells landed in the English trench. They poured out like ants from an antheap, and then we attacked. We crossed the fields at lightning speed and after many bloody hand-to-hand skirmishes we cleared the lot of them out of their trenches. Many came out with their hands up. Those who did not surrender were mowed down … To the left a few farms were still held by the enemy and we came under blistering fire. Comrades all around me collapsed. Then our madcap major arrived, smoking quite unconcernedly … every one of us who was worth his salt raced back to get reinforcements. When I returned I found the major lying on the ground with his chest torn open and a heap of bodies all around him … In four days our regiment had shrunk from three and a half thousand to six hundred. But we were all proud of having beaten the English.

D By the end of the war, aeroplanes were playing a much more significant role. However, not every flight ended in success.

1 What reasons can you find to explain why Operation Michael was a failure?
2 Why did the Kaiser have to abdicate?
3 What does source C suggest about Hitler's attitude towards the First World War?

THE WEIMAR REPUBLIC

A democratic republic

The war ended on 11 November 1918. The men who signed the armistice represented a new German government. The Germany which entered the war was an empire, led by a Kaiser who was almost a dictator. The new government was determined to introduce a parliamentary **democracy.** Why was this?

One reason was that President Wilson of America refused to offer peace to the Germans until it had a government which wanted democracy. At first the Kaiser had refused to abdicate. When mutinies and riots broke out in protest he finally agreed to do so. However, this meant that some Germans felt that democracy was being forced on Germany by her enemies.

The new government was not even able to rule from Berlin. The German capital was in the grip of a **communist** revolt (see page 8). So the government was forced to meet in the German town of Weimar. Its first job was to draw up a **constitution**. As a result, the period when Germany was ruled by a democratic constitution is known as Weimar Germany, even though the government soon moved back to Berlin. Elections were held and the Socialist, Friedrich Ebert, became the first ever President of Germany.

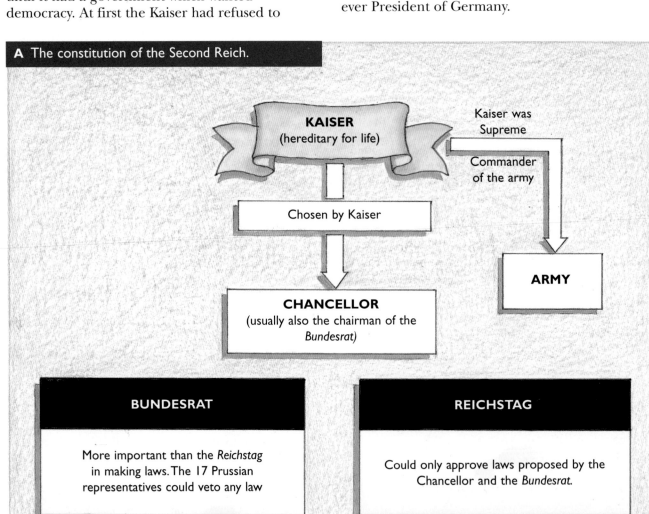

A The constitution of the Second Reich.

KAISER
(hereditary for life)

Kaiser was Supreme Commander of the army

Chosen by Kaiser

ARMY

CHANCELLOR
(usually also the chairman of the *Bundesrat)*

BUNDESRAT

More important than the *Reichstag* in making laws. The 17 Prussian representatives could veto any law

UPPER HOUSE OF PARLIAMENT

Members were chosen by the state governments of Germany

REICHSTAG

Could only approve laws proposed by the Chancellor and the *Bundesrat.*

LOWER HOUSE OF PARLIAMENT

Elected by all men over the age of 25. Fewer could vote in Prussia

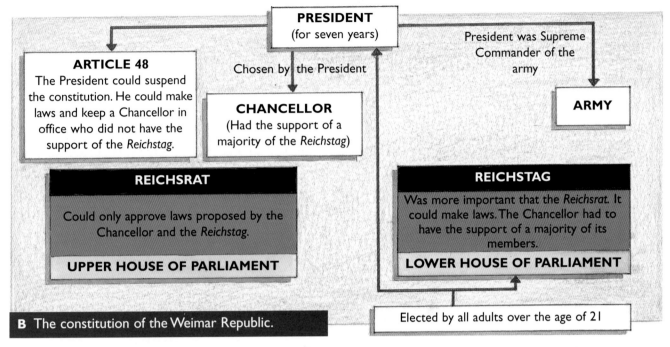

B The constitution of the Weimar Republic.

The diagram shows:

PRESIDENT (for seven years)

ARTICLE 48
The President could suspend the constitution. He could make laws and keep a Chancellor in office who did not have the support of the *Reichstag*.

Chosen by the President

CHANCELLOR
(Had the support of a majority of the *Reichstag*)

President was Supreme Commander of the army

ARMY

REICHSRAT
Could only approve laws proposed by the Chancellor and the *Reichstag*.
UPPER HOUSE OF PARLIAMENT

REICHSTAG
Was more important that the *Reichsrat*. It could make laws. The Chancellor had to have the support of a majority of its members.
LOWER HOUSE OF PARLIAMENT

Elected by all adults over the age of 21

The new constitution

Would the new constitution work? It certainly had some weaknesses which did cause problems:

1 Proportional representation. This was the voting system chosen for the *Reichstag* (parliament). It meant that if a party received five per cent of the votes, it also received five per cent of the seats in the Reichstag. This is a very fair system. However, it encourages lots of parties to be formed, since they all stand the chance of winning a few seats. This makes it nearly impossible for any one party to win the 51 per cent of the seats needed to form a government on their own. Therefore German governments tended to be **coalition** governments, made up of a number of parties. These coalitions seemed to work well in the 1920s. However, since parties have different aims the government can find it difficult to agree on certain decisions. The coalition government of the early 1930s found it difficult to deal with the Depression when the largest party, the **socialists**, wouldn't agree with the measures that the other members wanted to introduce (see page 15).

2 Article 48. This part of the constitution said that in an emergency the President could abandon democracy. Article 48 gave the President the power to pass laws without the agreement of the Reichstag. This is called 'rule by decree'. This is what happened in the early 1930s when the socialists left the government. The government ruled by decree, because it did not have enough support to get its laws passed by the Reichstag. It meant that the German people were more willing to accept Hitler's rule. He was not the first Chancellor to ignore the Reichstag.

3 The army. The new army, known as the *Reichswehr*, was only allowed to have 100 000 men. The generals in charge were the same men who had fought the war for the Kaiser. Many of them did not believe in democracy. They wanted the Kaiser to return so that they could be a large and powerful army once more.

4 The courts. The judges in the new Germany were also the same men who had been judges in the Second Reich. They had sympathy with people who wanted to end democracy. For instance, when Adolf Hitler was found guilty of treason in 1924 he received the minimum sentence – just five years' imprisonment. He only served nine months! (See page 19.)

1 Look at sources A and B.
   a) What were the differences between the Kaiser and the President?
   b) What were the similarities between the Kaiser and the President?
   c) Why was the Second Reich not a democratic system, even though the Reichstag was elected?
2 Look at source B and the text. Why might the Weimar constitution not stay democratic? (You will need to look at Article 48.)

The Effect of the Treaty of Versailles

Why did the German people react so strongly against the peace treaty?

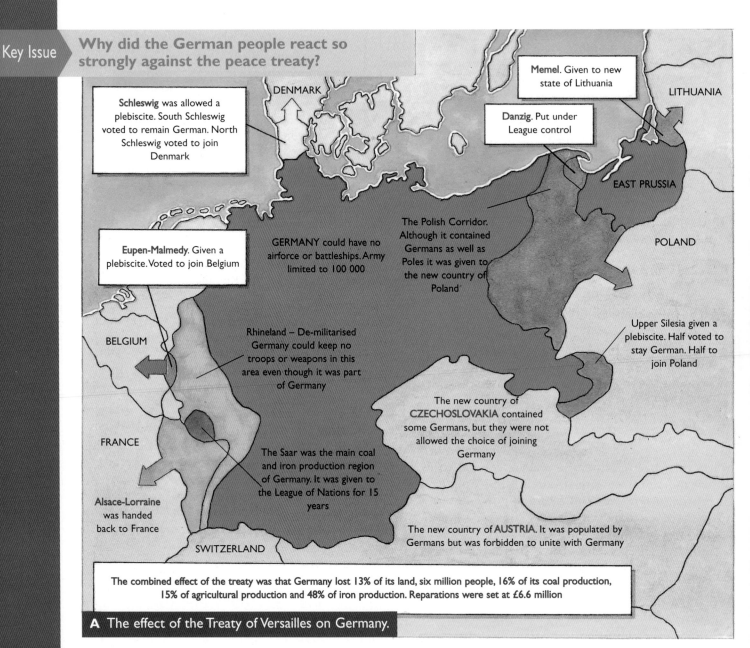

Schleswig was allowed a plebiscite. South Schleswig voted to remain German. North Schleswig voted to join Denmark

Memel. Given to new state of Lithuania

Danzig. Put under League control

DENMARK

LITHUANIA

EAST PRUSSIA

The Polish Corridor. Although it contained Germans as well as Poles it was given to the new country of Poland

POLAND

Eupen-Malmedy. Given a plebiscite. Voted to join Belgium

GERMANY could have no airforce or battleships. Army limited to 100 000

Upper Silesia given a plebiscite. Half voted to stay German. Half to join Poland

BELGIUM

Rhineland – De-militarised Germany could keep no troops or weapons in this area even though it was part of Germany

The new country of CZECHOSLOVAKIA contained some Germans, but they were not allowed the choice of joining Germany

FRANCE

The Saar was the main coal and iron production region of Germany. It was given to the League of Nations for 15 years

Alsace-Lorraine was handed back to France

The new country of AUSTRIA. It was populated by Germans but was forbidden to unite with Germany

SWITZERLAND

The combined effect of the treaty was that Germany lost 13% of its land, six million people, 16% of its coal production, 15% of agricultural production and 48% of iron production. Reparations were set at £6.6 million

A The effect of the Treaty of Versailles on Germany.

On 11 November 1918 the armistice was signed. It meant that Germany had surrendered. They were not allowed to take part in the peace negotiations. In June 1919 the terms of the peace treaty, known as the Treaty of Versailles, were announced. The German government was horrified by the terms. In total Germany lost 13 per cent of its territory, containing 48 per cent of its iron production and 15 per cent of its agricultural production as well as almost six million of its people. Germany also had to hand over 90 per cent of its merchant ships to make up for the losses caused by the U-boats. Look at source A. There were so many punishments. Germany was only allowed to have a small army of 100 000 men. None of them could be kept in the Rhineland, the area next to France. Germany couldn't have an airforce, and the navy couldn't have any battleships. Scheidemann resigned as Chancellor rather than accept the terms. However, Germany had to sign the treaty. If they didn't, the Allies would simply invade their country.

The stab in the back

The treaty left many German people feeling humiliated and wanting revenge for the way that the Allies had treated their country. The size of the **reparations** threatened to make every German poor. Many Germans blamed the new government for signing the armistice that had led to the treaty. They referred to the government as the 'November Criminals', a reference to the fact that the armistice was signed on 11 November. The government was accused of having stabbed the German army in the back. In other words the German army would have won the war if the armistice hadn't been signed. This, of course, was not true. However, the fact that many Germans came to believe this 'stab in the back' theory meant that the new democratic government was blamed for the humiliation of the Treaty of Versailles. It might have been more accurate to blame the Kaiser for leading Germany into the war, or the army leaders for losing the war. However, it was the government which was blamed.

B Fritz Ernst recalls, in 1966, how he felt about the Treaty of Versailles in 1918:

In our high school in Stuttgart, as indeed in most of the secondary schools in Germany after 1918, there was a noticeable rightist trend, which most of the teachers followed ... We believed it was a stab in the back that alone had prevented a German victory ... We did not know what the actual situation of the war had been in 1918; we were taught to hate the French and British and to despise the Americans.

C Ludendorff's evidence to a Reichstag committee after the war:

The war was now lost ... After the way our troops on the Western Front had been used up, we had to count on being beaten back again and again. Our situation could only get worse, never better.

Reparations

Worst of all was the 'war guilt' clause. This blamed the war entirely on Germany. In 1921 Germany was given a bill of £6600 million to repair the damage. Yet the British and French had probably done as much damage as the Germans.

At Versailles France did not just want Germany punished. They even hoped that Germany would be broken up.

D The reaction of a German newspaper, *Deutsche Zeitung*, in June 1919:

Vengeance! German nation! Today in the Hall of Mirrors [in the Palace of Versailles] the disgraceful Treaty is being signed. Do not forget it. The German people will, with unceasing work, press forward to reconquer the place among nations to which it is entitled. Then will come vengeance for the shame of 1919.

E A British historian, B J Elliott, writing in 1966:

The greatest weakness of the Treaty was that it did not end the German 'menace' by means of the punishment clauses. The German empire was left basically intact. Although Germany did lose some territories, by far the major part of her strength (land, population and resources) was untouched.

F In 1919 John Maynard Keynes resigned from the British delegation to Versailles because he thought the terms were far too harsh. Referring to the leaders who drew up the Treaty he wrote:

The future life of Europe was not their concern: its economy was not their anxiety. Their concerns, good and bad alike, related to frontiers and nationalities ... to the future weakening of a strong and dangerous enemy, to revenge. The victors shifted their unbearable financial burdens onto the shoulders of the defeated.

1 Look at source A. Make a list of all the punishments which the German people would have thought were unfair.
2 How might source B help to explain why so many Germans were willing to believe the 'stab in the back' theory?
3 'The Treaty of Versailles did not punish Germany enough.' Using the sources and text of this chapter explain whether you agree or disagree with this view.

Revolutions

Why were there so many revolts in the early years of Weimar Germany?

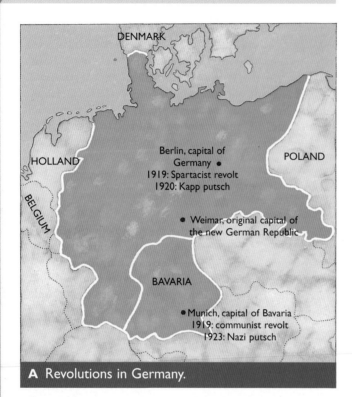

Berlin, capital of Germany ●
1919: Spartacist revolt
1920: Kapp putsch

HOLLAND

BELGIUM

DENMARK

POLAND

● Weimar, original capital of the new German Republic

BAVARIA

● Munich, capital of Bavaria
1919: communist revolt
1923: Nazi putsch

A Revolutions in Germany.

The early years of Weimar Germany were marked by a number of attempted **revolutions**. Although a democratic government was being set up in Germany, some Germans did not want democracy. Groups of these people tried to take control of the government of Germany by staging armed uprisings.

The Spartacists

These were a group of communists led by Karl Liebknecht and Rosa Luxemburg. They took their name from the Roman slave Spartacus who, 2000 years earlier, had led a slave revolt. The Spartacists were unhappy that the Second Reich was going to be replaced, they claimed, by another government controlled by rich people. With so many Germans starving they wanted a government which ruled on behalf of the poor, and which took away the wealth of the rich people. In 1917 the Bolsheviks had taken control of Russia. They had shown that a small group of communists could overthrow a government in a revolution. In January 1919 the Spartacists staged a revolution in Berlin. After two weeks the revolution was defeated. It was crushed

by the *Freikorps.* These were armed groups of ex-soldiers. The Weimar government decided to use them to put down the revolt. They did so with great brutality. Many communists, including Liebknecht and Luxemburg, were shot after they were captured.

Munich 1919

In April 1919 another group of communists managed to seize control of the government of Bavaria, the second biggest state in Germany. Again the German government used *Freikorps* to end the revolt.

The first two attempted revolutions were by extreme **left-wing** groups. Next came revolts by groups of the extreme **right-wing**.

B Starving people in Munich tear apart a dead horse in 1919.

The Kapp putsch

The *Freikorps* not only hated communism They also hated the humiliation of the Treaty of Versailles and the new German government which had signed it. In March 1920 a group of *Freikorps*, led by Dr Kapp, attempted to take power in Berlin. The *Freikorps* were also angry because the government had ordered all *Freikorps* units to disband. The army refused to stop Kapp and his 5000 followers. However, the workers of Berlin did not support the *Freikorps* and went on strike. Kapp and the *Freikorps* found that they could not govern Berlin and so the revolt ended.

'*Putsch*' means armed uprising in German.

C Dr Kapp explains what was wrong with Germany in 1919:

Prices are rising. Hardship is growing. Starvation threatens. The government lacks authority and is incapable of overcoming the danger. From the east we are threatened with destruction by communism.

D A German newspaper describes a parade by a group of *Freikorps*. This took place in March 1920, almost six months after the government had ordered all such groups to disband.

The Second Marine Brigade [of *Freikorps*] are crack troops that held firm against the enemy, both inside and outside of Germany. Full of patriotism, discipline, comradeship and loyalty to their leader, the brigade has given priceless, unselfish assistance to the present government in the maintenance of law and order.

E Groups of *Freikorps* with a tank. Their army equipment meant that they were too strong for the communists.

The Munich putsch

Between 1921 and 1923 there were many attempts by extreme groups to seize control of various German cities. They all failed. The most famous example came in November 1923 when Adolf Hitler tried to take control in Munich, the capital of Bavaria (see page 18). He failed because the police opposed him.

Assassinations

The right-wing groups not only tried to seize power, they also assassinated some of the 'November criminals'. In August 1921 Matthias Erzberger, the man who signed the armistice, was shot dead. In June 1922 the Foreign Minister Walter Rathenau was gunned down in Berlin.

Elections

The attempts to overthrow the Weimar government all failed. The first elections to the Reichstag (parliament) were held in 1920. Source F shows the result. It was not a good one for democracy. The Weimar republic had been created by the Socialist, Democratic and Centre Parties. If you add their results together you will see that they did not even win half of the seats. Clearly the German voters remained doubtful about their new system.

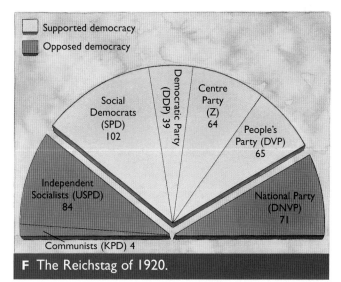

Supported democracy
Opposed democracy

Social Democrats (SPD) 102

Democratic Party (DDP) 39

Centre Party (Z) 64

People's Party (DVP) 65

Independent Socialists (USPD) 84

National Party (DNVP) 71

Communists (KPD) 4

F The Reichstag of 1920.

1 Look at source C. What reasons does Dr Kapp give for staging the revolt?
2 Look at source D. What do you think the paper is referring to in the phrase 'assistance to the present government in the maintenance of law and order'?
3 What impression of the Freikorps does source D give? Support your answer with evidence from the source.
4 Write a paragraph of 12–15 lines to explain why Germany was so difficult to govern in this period.

Why did Germany suffer from hyper-inflation in 1923?

The Ruhr invasion

By January 1923 Germany had fallen behind with reparation payments to Belgium and France. The French were angry because they needed the money to help to pay their war debts to the USA. Therefore French and Belgian troops were sent into the Ruhr, the industrial centre of Germany. The Ruhr is sited in the Rhineland so there were no German troops to stop the invading troops. The French and Belgians had decided to take the goods they needed, rather than wait for the Germans to send them.

B An English newspaper, *The Times* of 12 January 1923, describes the French troops entering the Ruhr city of Essen:

> At the head rode a party of cyclists in dark blue uniform and steel helmets, closely followed by five ... armoured cars. From these grim looking vehicles, of which the occupants were invisible, stood out the muzzles of machine guns, a silent threat to a sullen crowd. Many [of the Germans] took no trouble to hide the hatred in their hearts. Near the station I saw a 30-year-old man suddenly turn aside with a sob and mutter, 'The swine. My God, the pack of swine. May God pay them out for this cruel outrage'.

German resistance

The Germans could not use force to oppose the French and Belgians. Instead they chose passive resistance. The German workers in the Ruhr went on strike as a protest against the invasion. The strikers also took more direct action. They set some factories on fire. They sabotaged the pumps in some mines so that they flooded and could not be worked. Huge demonstrations were held in Ruhr cities to protest against the invasion. Some of these became violent. A number of strikers were shot by the French troops. The funerals became even bigger demonstrations. The French army arrested the entire police force of the Ruhr. They also stole money from banks and took equipment from offices and factories.

The results of the invasion

The invasion certainly united the German people in their hatred of the French and the Belgians. The strikers became heroes to the German people. They were standing up to the humiliating Treaty of Versailles and showing that Germany had not been crushed. The German government backed the strikers. They printed money to pay the strikers a wage. This of course increased inflation. The strike meant that even fewer goods were being produced in Germany and so this made inflation even worse. The extra strike money plus the collapse in production helped to turn the inflation into 'hyper-inflation'.

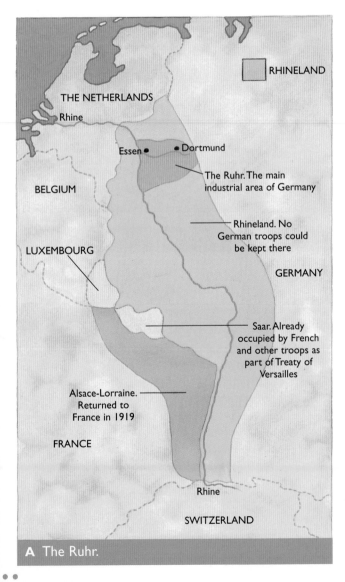

RHINELAND

THE NETHERLANDS

Rhine

Essen • • Dortmund

The Ruhr. The main industrial area of Germany

BELGIUM

Rhineland. No German troops could be kept there

LUXEMBOURG

GERMANY

Saar. Already occupied by French and other troops as part of Treaty of Versailles

Alsace-Lorraine. Returned to France in 1919

FRANCE

Rhine

SWITZERLAND

A The Ruhr.

C Hyper-inflation in action in July 1923. These clerks have come to collect money for their company's wages from the bank. Since goods kept their value better than money, by autumn 1923 the baskets would probably be worth more than the money they contained.

Hyper-inflation

The figure for German reparations had been set in 1921. It meant that Germany had to send large quantities of goods to France and Belgium as part of their payment. As a result there were not enough goods in Germany and prices rose. The German government also printed more money to pay both reparations and the workers. This just made inflation worse. In 1923 inflation suddenly shot out of control. In 1918 a loaf of bread had cost 60 pfennigs, that is 0.6 marks. By January 1923 it cost 250 marks and by September the price had rocketed to an unbelievable 1.5 million marks. Workers had to be paid twice a day and they brought wheelbarrows and suitcases so that they could carry home their wages. German money was almost worthless. Many people suffered. It was worst if you were on a fixed income, that is if there was no way you could increase your pay. An example would be a pensioner. If you had money in the bank then your life savings were wiped out.

However, not everyone suffered. Many businessmen did well. High inflation could lead to big profits, especially as the increase in wages did not keep pace with the increase in prices. Also many businessmen had borrowed money from the banks and these debts were wiped out. The rise in prices was also good for farmers. In a period of serious inflation food prices will always rise highest. People will give up buying less essential goods before they stop buying food! Foreigners who were in Germany suddenly found that they had a huge advantage. People who had dollars or pounds found that they could change them for millions of marks. They could afford things which ordinary Germans could not.

It became difficult to post a letter in 1923. There was not enough room to stick on all the stamps required to send it.

D A man remembers Germany in 1923:

In the summer of that inflation year my grandmother ... asked one of her sons to sell her house. He did so for I don't know how many million marks ... Nothing was left except a pile of worthless pieces of paper when she died a few months later.

E Another memory of 1923:

An acquaintance of mine, a clergyman, came to Berlin from the suburbs with his monthly salary to buy a pair of shoes for his baby; he could only buy a cup of coffee.

---

1 Why would many Germans feel desperate in 1923? (Look at sources D and E as well as the text.)
2 What reasons can you find to explain why foreigners were often very unpopular in Germany in 1923?
3 Why did Germany suffer from hyper-inflation in 1923? The table below gives three reasons. Draw the table and then explain how each of the reasons led to hyper-inflation.

Reason	Effect
1. Reparations.	
2. The invasion of the French and Belgian troops.	
3. The German government's support for the strikers.	

The Stresemann Years and the Collapse of the Weimar Republic

Why did Germany recover from the crisis of 1923? After such a recovery, what events caused the Republic to collapse?

Economic recovery

In 1923 the Germans suffered an invasion by foreign troops which they were powerless to stop. At the same time hyper-inflation destroyed the savings of millions of people. It seemed to be an ideal time for desperate people to turn their backs on democracy and instead support one of the extremist groups who were trying to seize power. Yet this did not happen. Why not?

Gustav Stresemann

One reason was certainly Gustav Stresemann. He became the new Chancellor in August 1923. Although he was the head of a coalition government this did not prevent him from taking decisive action. He introduced a new currency, the *Rentenmark*, to replace the old worthless mark. He ordered the striking workers of the Ruhr back to work and agreed that Germany should start to pay reparations again. This made him very unpopular with many Germans. It looked as though he was giving in to the countries which had defeated Germany in the war.

Stresemann was forced to give up the post of Chancellor in November 1923. The SPD, the largest party in the coalition, stopped supporting him. However, he became Foreign Minister in a new coalition government. In return for starting to pay reparations once more, Germany was rewarded with the introduction of the Dawes Plan in 1924. America agreed to lend Germany 800 million marks. The Germans could use this to build new factories which would produce jobs and goods which would raise the standard of living of the German people. The German reparation payments also helped America. Countries like France could use them to help them to pay back the huge amount of money which they had borrowed from America during the war. It also meant that France would have money to buy American goods. In 1925 the French and Belgian troops left the Ruhr. Democratic government was being successful and so the people were willing to continue to give democracy a chance.

Finally in 1929 the Young Plan was introduced, which reduced reparations by over 67 per cent.

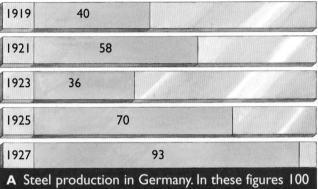

A Steel production in Germany. In these figures 100 stands for the steel production in 1913. Therefore a figure of 50 would mean that German production had dropped to half the amount produced in 1913.

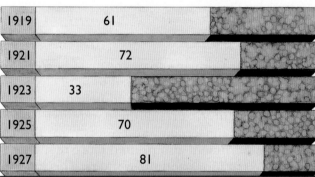

B Coal Production in Germany (100 stands for the coal production in 1913).

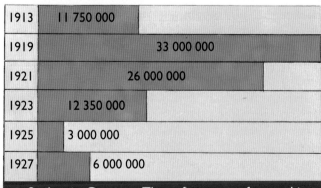

C Strikes in Germany. These figures are for working days lost. To arrive at this figure you have to multiply the number of people involved by the number of days they were on strike. In other words, 10 000 people on strike for five days would equal 50 000 working days lost.

A golden age?

Germany after 1923 became a very different place from Germany before 1923. People had money to spend. Berlin became the pleasure capital of Europe. Going to clubs and cafes became an important part of Berlin life. Artists flocked to Berlin. There was little **censorship**. People could do whatever they wanted.

> **D** Alec Swan, an Englishman, describes meeting girls in 1920s Berlin:
>
> When a girl wanted to pick you up, not a tart, just an ordinary girl in a shop, she used quite simply to bump into you, quite hard ... When a girl went back to your rooms, 'Shall we drink *first*?' was a standard opening line.

> **E** Alec Swan describes a Berlin gay club, El Dorado:
>
> The first person I saw was a Danish gentleman. Someone had spilled a champagne bucket down him and he was running gleefully across the floor, trousers hitched high ... At El Dorado it really was possible to mistake some of the regulars for beautiful women until you found yourself standing beside one in the urinal.

F A 1927 painting by George Grosz. He attacks the corrupt and pleasure-seeking life of Weimar Germany.

Foreign policy

The other countries began to treat Germany as an equal. In 1925 Germany and France signed the Treaty of Locarno in which they agreed never to try and change the border between them. In 1926 Germany was allowed to join the League of Nations. In 1928 Germany signed the Kellogg–Briand Pact with over 60 other countries. This said that these countries would never go to war against one another. In the same year Stresemann was awarded the Nobel Peace Prize. By the time he died in October 1929, it seemed that Stresemann had led Germany to a complete recovery from the disaster of the First World War.

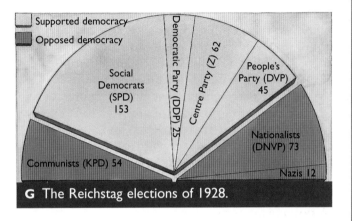

Supported democracy
Opposed democracy

Social Democrats (SPD) 153
Democratic Party (DDP) 25
Centre Party (Z) 62
People's Party (DVP) 45
Nationalists (DNVP) 73
Communists (KPD) 54
Nazis 12

G The Reichstag elections of 1928.

Q

1 What evidence can you find to support the statement that Berlin had become 'the pleasure capital of Europe'?

2 a) What does George Grosz (source F) think of life in Weimar Germany?
   b) Do you think sources D and E support his opinion?

3 Look at source G and compare it to source F on page 9. Then look at sources A, B and C in this unit. Do these sources support the statement that Stresemann 'had led Germany to a complete recovery'? To answer this you will need to look at the following questions.
   a) Add up the seats won by the parties which supported democracy in 1920 and in 1928. What does this suggest about the success of Stresemann's policies?
   b) Do sources A, B and C suggest that Germany was more prosperous by 1927 than it was in 1919? Explain your answer.
   c) Had other countries changed their view of Germany?

THE COLLAPSE OF THE WEIMAR REPUBLIC

Worldwide depression

On 24 October 1929 the Wall Street Crash occurred. This quickly created serious problems for Germany. The German economic boom had been based on loans from American banks. Because of the crisis in the USA these banks needed their money and so they demanded that Germany repay the loans. German industrial production slumped. Factories were producing less and so were forced to make some of their workers unemployed. This meant that there were fewer people with the money to buy goods and so factories sold still fewer goods. So even more workers were laid off. In 1928 there had been 1.4 million Germans unemployed. By 1931 this figure had leapt to 4.8 million. Not surprisingly many people lost faith in democracy when it could not provide them with a job. They turned to the extremist parties. When elections were held in 1930 both the Nazis and the communists did well. The communists promised a society where wealth was taken from the rich so that everyone else benefited. The Nazis promised to stop paying reparations, so that money could be used to create jobs.

By contrast the parties of the centre seemed to have no solution. Their coalition had saved Germany from economic disaster in 1923. This time the problem was much worse. The depression was worldwide. It was not simply a German problem. Unemployment continued to grow. Source C shows a Nazi view of the workers. They appear as helpless and desperate. Now look at source A. The government seemed to be able to do nothing to prevent more and more people from becoming unemployed.

Supported democracy

Opposed democracy

Democratic Party (DDP) 20

Centre Party (Z) 68

Social Democrats (SPD) 143

People's Party (DVP) 30

Nationalists (DNVP) 41

Communists (KPD) 77

Nazis (NSDAP) 107

B The results of the 1930 election.

C 'Our last hope' – a Nazi election poster. Hitler promised a solution to the problem of unemployment. As unemployment rose in Germany many people felt that the government parties had failed Germany.

1928 **1.8**

1929 **2.8**

1930 **3.2**

1931 **4.8**

1932 **6**

A German unemployment (figures in millions).

The government of Brüning

The Depression created serious problems for the government. With so many people without a job they had to pay out a large amount of money in unemployment benefit. However, with fewer people in work there were fewer people who were paying taxes. In other words the government simply didn't have enough money to pay the unemployed. To print money would have risked a return of hyper-inflation (see page 11). The government either had to cut the unemployment benefit or raise the taxes of those people who still had a job. In March 1930 Chancellor Brüning of the Centre Party proposed a 2.5 per cent tax increase on those people employed by the government. The SPD refused to agree to this and so left the government.

Even though he no longer had the support of the majority of the Reichstag, Brüning did not resign as Chancellor. Instead he introduced the increases using the decree (see page 5) of the President, Hindenburg. Soon afterwards he also cut unemployment benefit by five per cent and the pay of government employees by 23 per cent. All of these measures were introduced by presidential decree. The socialists would never have agreed to them. Whereas the coalition government had remained united in the face of the hyper-inflation of 1923, the government became divided when faced with the problems created by Depression.

The government of Papen

Faced with ever rising unemployment Brüning resigned in May 1932 and was replaced by von Papen. He called elections in July. He hoped that the parties which supported the government would be able to win a majority. Then they would be able to make laws democratically, rather than having to rely on presidential decree. It didn't work. Democratic government had left many people unemployed and discontented and so the voters turned in large numbers to a party which did not support democracy, the Nazi Party. They won 230 seats, far more than any other party. However, they had not got 50 per cent of the seats and so could not govern on their own. Von Papen continued as Chancellor and held new elections in November to try and win more seats. For a second time the tactic failed and von Papen was replaced as Chancellor by General von Schleicher. The Nazis, however, had managed to win 34 fewer seats. They were becoming less popular. In January 1933 General von Schleicher resigned because President Hindenburg refused to allow him to continue to govern by presidential decree. President Hindenburg then asked Adolf Hitler to become the new Chancellor.

Hitler as Chancellor

Hindenburg's role was crucial. Hitler would not have become Chancellor if the President had allowed General von Schleicher to govern by decree. The leaders of the Centre Party, such as von Papen, did not want General von Schleicher in power. They wanted to rule Germany and hoped to use the support of the Nazi Party to stay in power. They thought that they could dominate Hitler. Von Papen became Hitler's Vice-Chancellor. Ironically, Hitler became Chancellor at a time when it seemed that support for the Nazis was falling.

In 1925 Hindenburg became President with fewer than 50 per cent of the votes. The communists put up a candidate so splitting the majority anti-Hindenburg vote.

1 Look at source A, and then compare source B with source G on page 13.
   a) What happened to Nazi support between 1928 and 1930?
   b) What happened to German unemployment between 1928 and 1930?
   c) Why might the two be connected?
2 Do sources G on page 13 and B in this unit suggest that the German people believed in democracy? Look at what happened to the votes of the parties which did not believe in democracy.
3 'The Weimar Republic was doomed from the start.' Explain whether or not you agree with this interpretation using the material you have read so far. You will need to look at the following factors:
   ● the constitution;
   ● the Treaty of Versailles;
   ● the actions of German parties and politicians;
   ● the economic situation.

The Nazi Party

What did the Nazi party stand for?

In January 1933 Hitler became Chancellor. Yet only five years before the Nazis had been a small party which had won just 12 seats in the Reichstag. Who were the Nazis and what did they believe in?

A new party

In January 1919 Anton Drexler founded the German Workers' Party (DAP) in Munich. It was one of many new parties which sprang up in Germany at this time. In September 1919 Adolf Hitler joined the DAP. Together with Drexler he wrote the 25-point programme which stated the party's beliefs. These can be grouped into three main themes.

1 Nationalism. The DAP were one of a number of nationalist parties. They believed that Germany had been humiliated by the Treaty of Versailles. They believed that the German army had been stabbed in the back by the 'November Criminals'. They wanted all Germans to be united in a single country. One of the points in the programme stated: 'We demand the union of all Germans in a Greater Germany.'

2 Socialism. As they were a nationalist party, the DAP hated socialists and communists. Yet some of the 25 points in their programme were very similar to socialism. For instance, they demanded that workers should be able to share in company profits. They also wanted the government to take back any profits made by companies through supplying the war effort. Big companies should be **nationalised** and land should be shared out for the benefit of everyone.

> Hitler did not become a German citizen until 1932.

3 Anti-Semitism. The DAP were not just nationalists. They believed that the Germans were racially superior to all other people. Non-German people were inferior, known as *untermensch*, which means 'lesser people', and would not be citizens of the Reich. Jews were regarded as the lowest of all the non-German races. **Anti-Semitism** was not the creation of the Nazis. It was common among many of the extreme parties. It was especially common among Germans, like Hitler himself, who had not been born in Germany. Hitler blamed the Jews for most of Germany's problems (see page 52).

In 1920 the name of the party was changed to the National Socialist German Workers' Party, more usually known as the NSDAP or Nazis. In 1921 Hitler replaced Drexler as the leader.

A Hitler in the First World War (he is pictured on the far left).

The role of Hitler

Hitler had fought in the First World War and been awarded the Iron Cross, Germany's highest award for bravery. Like many others he felt that the bravery and self-sacrifice shown by people in the war needed to be recreated in peacetime if Germany was to be great again. Hitler believed that this required decisive leadership. He would be the man to provide that leadership. Therefore he set about turning the Nazis into a party with a large following. In 1920 the party bought its own newspaper so that it could put its views across to a greater number of people. Then Hitler created the *Sturm Abteilung* (SA) to attract more followers. In 1923 he tried to seize power in the Munich putsch.

The *Sturm Abteilung*

When the SA was formed in 1921 the Nazi newspaper, the *Volkischer Beobachter*, described it as the party's gymnastic and sports section. In fact it was mainly made up of ex-soldiers, the *Freikorps*. These were men who felt betrayed by the Weimar government. The SA offered them a new uniform in which to fight for Germany. They would disrupt the meetings of Hitler's opponents and often beat up opposition supporters. Their uniform was brown and so they were known as the 'Brownshirts'. SA headquarters was called the 'Brown House'. It was the SA who followed Hitler through the streets of Munich when he tried to take power.

B A Nazi poster of 1934. The SA man is shown as a heroic figure, worshipped by children and hated by Jews.

D An argument with Hitler, as reported by his supporter Otto Strasser.

'Power,' screamed Adolf, 'we must have power.'
'Before we gain it,' I replied firmly, 'let us decide what we propose to do with it ...'
Hitler ... thumped the table and barked, 'Power first! Afterwards we can act as we have to.'

E Hitler, writing in *Mein Kampf* in 1925:

It is easier for a camel to pass through the eye of a needle than a great man be discovered by an election.

1 Name two ways in which the First World War helped to create Nazi ideas.
2 How do sources B and C help to explain the popularity of the SA?
3 a) What is Hitler saying about democracy in source E?
   b) How does this help to explain why Hitler attempted to seize power in 1923? (See pages 18–19.)

C The SA parade at the 1933 Party Rally.

The Munich Putsch

Why did Hitler attempt to seize power? Why did he fail?

A A group of SA in Munich in 1923. They are using the flag of the Second Reich.

B Hitler speaking about the German government in April 1923:

In the near future, when we have gained power, we shall have the further duty of taking these creatures of ruin ... these traitors to the state, and hanging them to the gallows to which they belong.

C A police report of the events of the meeting on 8 November.

Hitler returned [to the side room], this time without a pistol. He talked about his second speech and the jubilation it had produced and he pressed the gentlemen further. Suddenly Ludendorff entered the room in a hat and coat and, without asking any questions, with obvious excitement and with a trembling voice, declared, 'Gentlemen, I am just as surprised as you are. But the step has been taken, it is a question of the Fatherland [Germany] and the great national and racial cause, and I can only advise you, go with us and do the same.' ... After long urging Kahr declared 'I am willing to take over the destiny of Bavaria.'

8 November

By November 1923 the state of Bavaria was under the control of Gustav von Kahr. On 8 November he was to address a public meeting at the Bürgerbräu beer hall. With him was General von Lossow, the commander of the Bavarian army. At 8.30 pm the hall was surrounded by the SA and Hitler entered with an armed escort. A machine-gun was set up by the SA at the back of the hall. Hitler announced that Kahr and Lossow were under arrest. Ludendorff, who had commanded the German army at the end of the war, also joined in. After private discussions in a side room

Kahr agreed to lead Hitler's takeover of power. Kahr and Lossow were then allowed to go home – an important mistake.

What was Hitler trying to do? Why had he taken control of the government of Bavaria? Hitler hoped that by doing so he would soon be able to take control of the whole of Germany. He believed the time was right. Many Germans felt that the government had betrayed the German people by signing the Treaty of Versailles. In 1923 the government had betrayed them again. Stresemann had given in to the French and agreed to resume paying reparations. Most Germans had wanted the strike in the Ruhr to continue. Hyper-inflation (see page 11) also meant that people were unhappy and ready for change. Hitler believed that the German people wanted a new, strong government.

9 November

Hitler was copying the example of the Italian fascist leader, Mussolini. In 1922 he had led the March on Rome to seize power in Italy. However, Mussolini had the support of the Italian king and so the Italian army did not stop Mussolini's blackshirts from marching into Rome. Hitler soon discovered the situation was very different in Munich. Once he was out of the beer hall General von Lossow organised the army to stop Hitler. Kahr, now that he was free, supported von Lossow. In the afternoon Hitler, Ludendorff and their supporters set off on a march through Munich. They had few weapons. 2000 rifles which had been secretly supplied by the German army had no firing pins. In the Odeonplatz they were met by a group of Bavarian state troopers. In the fight that followed 16 Nazis were killed along with four troopers. Hitler's colleague Göring was seriously wounded. Ludendorff was arrested at the scene. Hitler was arrested 48 hours later.

> **D** Lt Freiherr von Godin, who was in charge of a company of Bavarian state troopers, reported:

> **Suddenly a Hitler man who stood a pace away to my left fired a pistol at my head. The shot missed and killed Sgt Hollweg behind me. For a fraction of a second my company stood completely frozen. Then, before I could give an order, my people opened fire, a volley in effect. At the same time the Hitler people started to fire and for twenty or thirty seconds a real fire fight was on.**

The results of the putsch

It could be argued that the most successful part of the putsch was the trial. Ludendorff was declared to be innocent. Hitler admitted that he was guilty of trying to overthrow the Weimar system of parliamentary government. He then set about showing how this was no crime since he was trying to restore German greatness. Many Germans felt this was a convincing argument. The trial gave

Hitler a national audience. Hitler was sentenced to five years in prison, though he actually served only nine months. While in prison he wrote *Mein Kampf (My Struggle)*, which set out his ideas (see page 16). It also gave Hitler the opportunity to reflect on the reasons for the failure of the putsch. In future the Nazis would try to win power by legal means. They would win votes rather than take power by force.

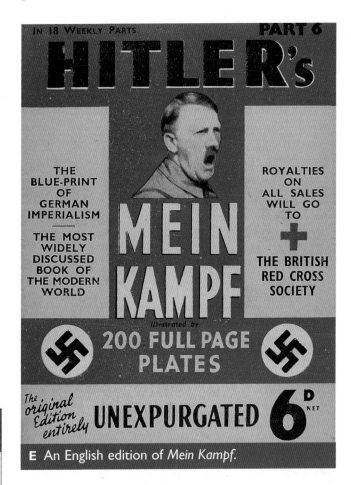

IN 18 WEEKLY PARTS — PART 6

HITLER's

THE BLUE-PRINT OF GERMAN IMPERIALISM

THE MOST WIDELY DISCUSSED BOOK OF THE MODERN WORLD

ROYALTIES ON ALL SALES WILL GO TO ✛ THE BRITISH RED CROSS SOCIETY

MEIN KAMPF

Illustrated by

200 FULL PAGE PLATES

The original Edition entirely **UNEXPURGATED** **6**D NET

E An English edition of *Mein Kampf*.

Q

1 Who are the traitors of the state that Hitler is referring to in source B?
2 a) Ludendorff was found innocent of trying to overthrow the government at his trial. Does source C support this verdict? Explain your answer.
   b) Why do you think that Hitler was found guilty but Ludendorff was not?
3 Why was General von Lossow's role crucial to the outcome of the putsch?
4 What evidence can you find that the putsch was badly planned?

The Nazi Party: Growth and Victory

What sort of supporters did the Nazis attract?

Who voted for the Nazis?

The view expressed in source A is a common one. There were many discontented people in Germany, especially among the working class. Once Hitler was able to get his message over to them, providing simple and easily understood policies, then it was inevitable that he would take power. He was the right man in the right place. Yet is this true?

A Hugh Thomas, an English writer in 1995:

> But once ... Hitler's rabble rousing ... had fascinated the working class, and once they had been provided with ready scapegoats such as the Jews, Hitler's takeover of power was almost inevitable.

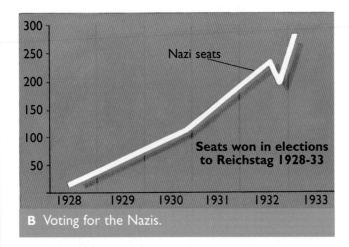

B Voting for the Nazis.

(graph: Nazi seats / Seats won in elections to Reichstag 1928-33; vertical axis 0–300, horizontal axis 1928–1933)

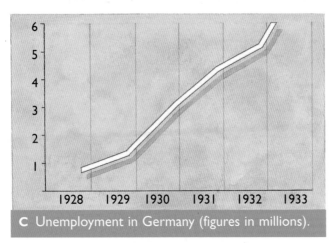

(graph: vertical axis 1–6, horizontal axis 1928–1933)

C Unemployment in Germany (figures in millions).

Did the workers vote for the Nazis?

It would seem from sources B and C that as more people lost their jobs they were willing to vote for the Nazis. However, if we look more closely at the evidence a different picture begins to appear. The workers who were losing their jobs had traditionally voted for the socialists, who had helped to gain them better wages and working conditions. If these workers no longer wanted democracy, the Communist Party offered them a more obvious alternative than the Nazis. The Socialist Party, the SPD, wanted to bring about socialism by winning elections. The communists stood for achieving socialism through revolution.

> By claiming to stand for morality and family values the Nazis were able to convince many women to vote for them.

The election of 1928

Seats	Party
54	Communist Party (KPD)
152	Socialist Party (SPD)
79	Nationalist Party (DNVP)
13	Nazi Party (NSDAP)
175	others

The election of July 1932

Seats	Party
89	Communist Party (KPD)
133	Socialist Party (SPD)
40	Nationalist Party (DNVP)
230	Nazi Party (NSDAP)
117	others

D The elections of 1928 and 1932 (number of seats).

As you will have seen from sources D and E, the total left-wing vote did not decline during the Depression. So it was not the industrial working class in the big cities who were voting for the

Nazis. They continued to vote for the socialists and the communists. While the Nazis received almost 38 per cent of the vote in the whole of Germany in 1932 they only got 28 per cent in the Ruhr, the main industrial area of Germany. In contrast the communists won as much as 70 per cent of the votes in some Ruhr towns. We need to look elsewhere for the new Nazis. They are to be found in three very different areas .

Who was voting for the Nazis?

1 The countryside

It was in rural areas of Germany that the Nazis first became popular after 1923. Although the German economy recovered quickly from hyper-inflation, agricultural prices slumped. Remember that food prices had been very high in 1923. Farmers were unhappy that they were suffering when other people were doing well. These farmers turned to the Nazis.

E 'We farmers are clearing out the muck'. A Nazi poster of 1932 shows the 'muck' as socialists and Jews.

2 The middle classes

In particular, middle class people who worked for the government were very likely to vote for Hitler.

This is hardly surprising after the government of Brüning had cut their wages by 23 per cent at the same time as they had raised their taxes. Middle-class people who did not work for the government also voted for the Nazis. They feared that the unemployed working class might lead a communist revolution which would destroy the middle class.

3 The working class outside the big cities

We have seen that the workers in the cities did not vote for the Nazis in large numbers. These workers were usually members of trade unions who continued to support the socialists and communists. However, outside the big cities most workers worked for small family firms. They did not belong to unions and now were likely to vote for the Nazis.

F Heinrich Galm, a communist, describes the town of Offenbach just days after the Nazi election victory in 1933. Offenbach had no large factories.

I could not recognise the town. Offenbach under the swastika! Swastika flags [the Nazi symbol] everywhere. The marketplace was astonishing. We went down the Biergrund into the workers' districts where our votes used to come from ... swastikas in every window.

1 Compare sources B and C. What impression do they give for the reasons why more and more people were voting for the Nazis?
2 What was the combined vote for the left-wing parties (KPD and SPD) in 1928?
3 What was the combined vote for the left-wing parties in 1932?
4 Do these figures support the view expressed in source A that it was the working class – the traditional supporters of the SPD and KPD – who were now voting for the Nazis? Explain your answer.
5 a) What impression of working-class voting is given in source F?
   b) How can you explain this?

Extended writing
In source A Hugh Thomas says that the working class became 'fascinated' by Hitler's message. In other words he believes that they were more likely to be attracted to Hitler and the Nazis than to other groups. Do you agree with his interpretation? Use the evidence from this section to support your argument.

VICTORY

Why was Hitler able to come to power in 1933 when he had failed in 1923?

Hitler became Chancellor in January 1933. Almost ten years earlier, in November 1923, he had failed to take control of Bavaria. Why was he so much more successful the second time around?

Look back to pages 18–19. Hitler had tried to seize power by using force in 1923. The Bavarian army had been ordered to stop him. The leaders of Bavaria were against him. Now look back to pages 20–21. In 1933 the Nazis were the largest political party in Germany. The German President, Hindenburg, actually asked Hitler to take power. After the failure of the Munich putsch Hitler had decided to change tactics. His success in 1933 showed that his decision had been the right one.

Propaganda

It was not simply Hitler's change of tactics which led to his victory. By 1932 Hitler was also a nationally known politician, whereas in 1923 he was only known in Bavaria. During the election campaigns he used posters and mass meetings to hammer home his message. He flew across Germany to address meetings in every major city.

In the spring of 1932 he stood for President against the now 84-year-old war hero, Hindenburg. Although Hitler was defeated he gained a very respectable 13 million votes and, since Hindenburg did not campaign, Hitler had the whole of Germany listening to him.

Wealthy backers

Hitler could not have afforded these campaigns without the help of wealthy backers. Many powerful businessmen, such as the steel manufacturer Thyssen and the armaments manufacturer Krupp, were willing to lend their support to Hitler. Weimar Germany had seen the growth in the power of the trade unions and an increase in the wages and better working conditions of working people. With Germany in a depression businessmen wanted to cut wages and benefits. Hitler promised to destroy the trades unions and give businessmen a free hand. Therefore, many businessmen were willing to give Hitler money. They believed that they would be better off in a Germany led by Hitler.

The Weimar constitution

As mentioned on pages 4–5 the electoral system in Weimar Germany was proportional representation. This led to coalition governments made up of a number of parties. No one party ever won enough

A The SA celebrate Hitler's victory in front of the Brandenburg Gate in Berlin. This picture was painted five years later, in 1938. What impression is it trying to give?

votes to form a government on their own. For much of the Weimar period Germany was ruled by a 'Grand Coalition' made up of most of the parties which supported democracy. In 1930 the largest party, the socialists (SDP), left the government (see page 15). This forced the government to rule by presidential decree. When President Hindenburg finally decided to stop this, the coalition needed a party with enough support to give it a majority. Since the SPD wouldn't rejoin the government, the Nazis offered the only alternative. President Hindenburg did not really believe in democracy, so he did not mind appointing Hitler as Chancellor. The system of proportional representation helped Hitler to come to power.

The Depression

Proportional representation only helped Hitler because the Nazis were the largest party. Hitler's prospects had been changed by the Depression. It was not simply that six million people became unemployed. Many others feared for their future.

They worried that they might soon lose their jobs too. Others feared that a communist revolution would take place. The middle classes feared that this would destroy their position in society and take away their wealth. A very wide range of people decided to vote for the Nazis. The other parties seemed to have failed. The Nazis had the advantage of never having been in government. They hadn't yet failed, so many people were willing to overlook the brutal SA and give the Nazis a chance.

C The historian, T. Childers, explains the support for the Nazis :

Yet, even at the height of its popularity, the Nazis position as a people's party was weak at best. If the party's support was a mile wide, it was an inch deep ... It remains one of history's most tragic situations that at precisely the moment when the Nazis were beginning to lose votes, Hitler was installed as Chancellor by politicians who had done so much to undermine the democracy in Germany.

A·I·Z

ERSCHEINT WÖCHENTLICH EINMAL • PREIS 20 PFG., Kč 1.60
30 GR., 30 SCHWEIZER RP. • V. b. b. • NEUER DEUTSCHER
VERLAG, BERLIN W8 • JAHRGANG XI • NR 42 • 16.10.1932

DER SINN DES HITLERGRUSSES:

Motto:
MILLIONEN
STEHEN
HINTER MIR!

Kleiner Mann bittet um große Gaben

B 'The meaning of the Hitler salute – millions stand behind me.' A 1932 anti-Hitler poster by John Heartfield (see page 44).

Q

1 Look at source B.
   a) What is the artist suggesting about Hitler's support?
   b) Why was this likely to be the case?
2 What other reasons can you find to explain the growth in support for the Nazi party?
3 Read source C.
   a) What election is the author referring to when he says that the Nazis were losing votes?
   b) What does Childers mean by the phrase 'the party's support was a mile wide'?
   c) What does he mean by 'it was an inch deep'?

Extended writing
Childers believed that Hitler had been brought to power by politicians who did not believe in democracy. Do you agree with this interpretation?
To answer this question you will need to look at a number of areas such as:
- the level of support for the Nazis;
- Hitler's tactics;
- the Weimar constitution;
- the Depression;
- the actions of the other political leaders.

9

Setting up a Dictatorship

How did the Nazis secure their hold on power? Was the Reichstag fire deliberately planned to help them win the election? Why were the leaders of the SA killed in 1934?

A A 1933 poster showing Hitler alongside Hindenburg. Beneath them are the old Imperial German flag and the Nazi swastika.

Elections

Although Hitler became the Chancellor of Germany he was only the leader of a coalition government. Only two members of his government were fellow Nazis, the First World War flying ace Hermann Göring and Wilhelm Frick. So he called new elections in the hope that he could win more than 50 per cent of the vote in order to rule without other parties. He did have advantages which no previous Chancellor had enjoyed. Göring was the Prussian Minister of the Interior. This meant that he controlled the police in about two-thirds of Germany. The police were instructed to leave the SA alone This meant that the Nazis were able to attack their opponents without being arrested. In February the Reichstag building burnt down (see page 26). Hitler used this as an excuse to arrest leading communists and so make it far

more difficult for the KPD to win. Despite all of these advantages the Nazis still only won 44 per cent of the vote in the election of March 1933.

In the next few months Hitler established a dictatorship in Germany. A dictatorship is a government where no opposition is allowed. The government is able to do whatever it wants. One by one Hitler removed all possible sources of opposition.

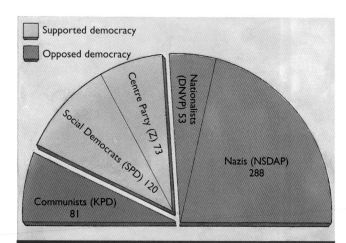

- Supported democracy
- Opposed democracy

Social Democrats (SPD) 120

Centre Party (Z) 73

Nationalists (DNVP) 53

Nazis (NSDAP) 288

Communists (KPD) 81

B The election of March 1933.

Removing opposition to the Nazis

1 The Enabling Act

In the Reichstag there were 485 MPs who belonged to parties which opposed the Nazis. Hitler could only rule with the support of the Nationalists, the DNVP. Hitler got round this problem with the Enabling Act. This gave Hitler the power to make any law he wanted without needing a vote in the Reichstag. It might seem surprising that the members of the Reichstag would agree to this. However, it should be remembered that governments had been ruling in a similar way for the last three years when they had ruled through presidential decree. Also Hitler had banned the KPD so that they couldn't vote against the Enabling Act. Many people were happy to see the communists banned. The middle classes were afraid of a communist revolution. They blamed the communists for the increased violence on the streets of German towns, even though much of it was carried out by the SA and the similar nationalist group, the *Stahlheim*.

2 Political parties

The KPD were the first party to be banned. The other parties soon followed. In May the socialist SPD were banned. In July the other parties, some of whom had helped Hitler to become Chancellor, were also banned. A Law Against the Formation of Parties was also passed. The NSDAP was now the only party in Germany. The leaders of the communists and the socialists were arrested and put in concentration camps. The first of these camps was opened at Dachau in March 1933. It was not just the leaders who were arrested. Of the 300 000 Germans who were members of the KPD in January 1933 half would end up in the concentration camps. 30 000 of them would die there.

3 Trade unions

The trade unions were very closely associated with the left-wing parties and so natural opponents of the Nazis. In May all trade unions were abolished. Strikes were made illegal.

4 Regional government

Remember that Germany had only been founded in 1871. The once independent countries that joined the new Germany became states or *Länder*. These were run by elected governors. Many of these governors opposed Hitler's policies. In April 1933 Hitler replaced these elected governors with Reich governors who were appointed by Hitler. All were Nazis.

> Hitler called his new Germany the Third Reich, the third German Empire. He promised that it would last for one thousand years. It lasted for just twelve.

C Hitler receives the congratulations of the SA at the Nuremberg Party Rally in 1933.

Führer

Hitler had now achieved almost complete control of Germany. Only the aged President Hindenburg could stop him. The President could sack a Chancellor and replace him with someone else. In July 1934 Hindenburg died. Hitler took over and combined the offices of Chancellor and President. In future he was to be known as *Führer*, which means 'leader.' On 2 August the German army swore allegiance to Hitler as *Führer*, rather than to Germany. Hitler now had complete control. Germany was a dictatorship.

D Hindenburg reflects on the first 12 months of Nazi rule in a letter to Hitler in March 1934:

Much has happened in the past year with regard to the removal of economic distress and the rebuilding of the Fatherland [Germany] ... I am confident that in the coming year you and your fellow workers will successfully continue ... the great work of reconstruction which you have so energetically begun, on the basis of the new happily achieved national unity of the German people.

Q

1 Look at source A.
   a) Why do you think that the Nazis issued a poster showing Hitler beside Hindenburg?
   b) What sort of people might vote for Hitler as a result of this poster?
2 Does source D support the image shown in source A? Give your reasons.
3 In source D Hindenburg refers to 'the new happily achieved national unity of the German people'. Do you agree with his view? What evidence can you find in the text to support your opinion?
4 Do you think it is correct to describe Nazi Germany as a dictatorship? Give your reasons.

Extended writing
'Hitler was able to make himself dictator because of the mistakes of others rather than his own political ability.' Explain whether or not you agree with this interpretation by referring to the following points (as well as others which you feel are relevant):
- the attitude of von Papen in 1932;
- Hindenburg's decision to ask Hitler to be the Chancellor;
- Hitler's policies as Chancellor;
- the Enabling Act and how it was passed.

THE REICHSTAG FIRE

A The burnt out ruins of the Reichstag building.

B 'A battle for Germany.' This Nazi poster was issued in 1933. It shows the work of the SA as a battle against the communists.

C Van der Lubbe in a statement to police:

As to the question whether I acted alone, I declare absolutely that this was the case. No one helped me at all.

D Rudolf Diels, the Head of the Berlin police at the time, commented:

Why should not a single match be enough to set fire to the cold yet inflammable splendour of the chamber, the old upholstered furniture, the heavy curtains, and the bone dry wooden panelling! But this specialist had used a whole knapsack full of inflammable material. He had been so active that he had laid several fires.

The Reichstag was the German parliament building. It was a symbol of democracy in Germany. In March 1933 Reichstag elections were to be held. Hitler hoped to get 50 per cent of the votes so that the Nazis could rule Germany without coalition partners. On the evening of 27 February 1933 the Reichstag building burnt down. Who was responsible?

The authorities were in no doubt. A young Dutch communist, Marinus van der Lubbe, was arrested at the Reichstag. He was carrying matches and firelighters. As source C shows, van der Lubbe admitted that he was guilty.

There would seem to be little problem . The criminal had been caught red-handed and had confessed. Yet van der Lubbe's story did not convince everyone. Hitler and Göring didn't believe he had acted alone. They declared that it was part of a communist plot to overthrow democracy. Leading communists were put in prison.

E A British journalist, D Sefton Delmer, was an eye-witness to Göring's and Hitler's reactions:

Five minutes after the fire had broken out I was outside the Reichstag watching the flames licking their way up the great dome into the tower. A cordon had been flung around the building and no one was allowed to pass it.

After about twenty minutes of fascinated watching I suddenly saw the famous black motor car of Adolf Hitler slide past, followed by another car containing his personal bodyguard. I rushed after them and was just in time to attach myself to the fringe of Hitler's party as they entered the Reichstag ...

Captain Göring, his right hand man ... joined us in the lobby. He had a flushed and excited face. 'This is undoubtedly the work of the communists, Herr Chancellor,' he said. 'A number of communist deputies [MPs] were present here in the Reichstag twenty minutes before the fire broke out. We have succeeded in arresting one of the arsonists.'

Was it really a communist plot? British newspapers of the time were not convinced, as the report of the trial given in source F shows.

F The *Daily Telegraph*, 6 December 1933

The reasoned judgement in the Reichstag fire trial, which was read by the judge, Dr Bünger, at Leipzig on Saturday, fell into two sections ... The first part of the judgement was a clear and even ruthless analysis of the evidence .... Van der Lubbe is guilty of treason, the act being arson with intent to bring about a revolution ... Lubbe could not possibly have fired the Reichstag alone but his accomplices are unknown ...

The second portion of the judgement was more like an election speech than a legal opinion. A highly controversial attack on the Communist Party, it was evidently intended to appease the wilder Nazis. Their views have been put forward on more than one occasion during the trial and their spokesmen are General Göring and the notorious Breslau Chief of Police Lt Heines.

If the German court had got it right, just who were these unknown accomplices who had helped van der Lubbe to start the fire? Did it require more than one person to set light to so many fires? At the end of the war important Nazis, who had been captured, were put on trial. After his trial Göring committed suicide. As source G shows, General Halder gave evidence that Göring was responsible for the Reichstag fire. But he was not a trusted adviser of Hitler in 1943, so would he have been at the lunch? In 1942 he had been replaced as Chief of Staff after disagreeing with Hitler over the invasion of Russia.

G General Halder, in evidence to the Nuremberg War Crimes trials in 1946:

On the occasion of a lunch on the Führer's birthday in 1943, the people around the Führer turned the conversation to the Reichstag building and its artistic value. I heard with my own ears how Göring broke into conversation and shouted: 'The only one who really knows [about] the Reichstag is I, for I set fire to it'.

H Hermann Göring, in evidence to the Nuremberg War Crimes trials in 1946:

What the general [Halder] says is not true ... The whole thing is preposterous. Even if I had started the fire, I would most certainly not have boasted about it.

I The British historian, A J P Taylor, writing in 1961:

The Nazis had nothing to do with the burning of the Reichstag. The young Dutchman, van der Lubbe, did it all alone, exactly as he claimed.

So exactly who did burn down the Reichstag? Is source I right? Did van der Lubbe tell the truth all along? Or did the Nazis merely want an excuse to ban the communists and so win the next election? The evidence is far from complete but like any historian you have now got to decide which evidence you trust the most and which you will choose to reject.

1 Why does Diels (source D) say that he believed van der Lubbe?
2 Do you think that source D is reliable evidence if we wish to discover who burnt down the Reichstag?
3 Does source C support the conclusion of source F? Give your reasons?
4 According to source F, does the court support the view of source E or not?
5 Do you believe the interpretation given in source I? Did van der Lubbe burn down the Reichstag on his own?
6 Even if the Nazis weren't responsible for the fire, they certainly benefited from it. In what ways do you think they benefited?

THE NIGHT OF THE LONG KNIVES

In the early hours of 30 June 1934 Hitler entered a hotel in the Bavarian resort of Bad Wiessee. He was accompanied by a group of heavily armed SS, his bodyguards. Staying at the hotel were many important members of the SA, including Ernst Röhm, the leader. Hitler told Röhm and the other SA leaders that they were under arrest. They were taken to Munich where they were shot. Over the next few days other leading members of the SA, such as Gregor Strasser, were also arrested by the SS and shot. Up to 200 people were killed, including politicians such as former Chancellor Kurt von Schleicher, who were not Nazis let alone members of the SA. These events have become known as 'The Night of the Long Knives'. What was going on? Why did it happen? Who was involved?

The SA

The SA had long been the public face of the Nazis, beating up communists and holding large meetings and demonstrations. By 1934 there were probably two million of these 'brownshirts'. Many of them had been unemployed. Now that Hitler was in power they expected him to take wealth from the rich. The SA leader demanded that the SA should also take over the army. He believed that the SA should become the focus of a National Socialist Germany.

The SS

The SS, the *Schutzstaffel*, had been formed in 1925 as Hitler's personal bodyguard. They were technically part of the SA. However their leader, Heinrich Himmler, wanted them to become a separate organisation. Late in the evening of 28 June he told Hitler that Röhm and the SA were planning to seize power immediately and replace Hitler. Röhm's statements, such as source C, probably made this believable to Hitler. It was after Himmler's warning that Hitler set off for Bad Wiessee to arrest the SA leaders.

The army

The army was dominated by men who had fought in the Kaiser's army in the First World War. They believed that Hitler was the only leader in Germany who would allow them to ignore the Treaty of Versailles and re-arm. Under Hitler they could become a powerful, modern army. However, they were frightened by the thought that they might be taken over by the SA.

A The SA parade at Nuremberg in 1933. In Hitler's Germany impressing the people would be their main role.

Industrialists

Many leading industrialists, such as Fritz Thyssen the powerful steel magnate, supported Hitler. They feared communism. They believed that Hitler was the one leader who could be relied upon to destroy the communists. However, like von Papen in source C, they feared that the SA programme looked far too much like communism.

Hitler

Now that Hitler was in power he wanted to create a Greater Germany and gain *Lebensraum* or 'living space' in the east. This would require a strong and powerful army. So it was important to him that he had the support of the army. He also needed the support of the industrialists. They would need to create the wealth which would pay for the army as well as actually manufacturing the weapons. In contrast Hitler only needed the SA to take part in huge parades, like that shown in source B, to impress the German people.

Göring

Hermann Göring was in charge of the arrests and assassinations in Berlin. Like Röhm he had taken part in the Munich putsch and so was a Nazi hero. Göring was extremely ambitious. The removal of important Nazis like Röhm would make him even more powerful.

What were the results?

* One undoubted result was that many opponents of Hitler were now dead. It was not just Röhm. Other leading Nazis who agreed with Röhm's views, such as Gregor Strasser, were also killed. Hitler had also murdered conservative

opponents such as General von Schleicher. These were men who might have won the support of the army and the industrialists.

* On 20 June 1934 the SS was established as a separate organisation from the SA. Himmler now took orders only from Hitler.

* A month later the army swore an oath promising to be loyal to Hitler. In the past the army had sworn an oath to be loyal to Germany.

* Murder had now become a part of government action. Hitler had simply wiped out 200 of his political opponents and no one stopped him. Hindenburg backed him, as did the Reichstag. When he went to the Reichstag to explain his actions, Hitler said that there were no trials because Hitler himself had acted as the 'Supreme Judge of the German people'. Dictatorship had begun.

E The new Oath of Allegiance, which was taken by the army after the Night of the Long Knives.

'I swear before God to give my total obedience to Adolf Hitler, Führer of the Reich and of German people, and I pledge my word as a brave soldier to observe this oath always, even at the peril of my life.

Q

1 Look at source D. Who are the men with their arms raised?
2 Why does it say 'the double cross' on Hitler's sleeve? What else can you find in the cartoon which is making a similar point?
3 Himmler told Hitler that the SA were planning to seize power. Do the actions of the SA leaders on 30 June support this view? Does source B support Himmler's accusation? Explain your answer.
4 Who gained and who lost from the Night of the Long Knives? To answer this question you will need to look at:
* Hitler;
* Himmler and the SS;
* Göring;
* the army;
* the SA;
* industrialists.
Remember that some groups or individuals may have gained as well as lost.

D 'They salute with both hands now.' A British cartoon from 1934.

The Hitler Myth

Why was it that the German people were willing to put up with the violence and injustice which followed the Night of the Long Knives? In the main this was due to the myth that was created. Hitler was presented as a near god-like leader – an ordinary soldier who had risen to become the symbol of the nation and the creator of a new Germany. Every decision he made was the right one for the country. There is no question that Hitler was incredibly popular. These pages show five reasons for the success of the myth. His foreign and economic policies were successful. Unlike previous leaders Hitler seemed to deliver what he promised. Propaganda and education convinced people that Nazi views were right. Terror made sure that opposition was crushed.

The fact that Hitler was not married was used to help to build the myth. Here was a man who gave up personal happiness in the service of his country. Hitler's mistress, Eva Braun, was kept hidden from the people.

A Hitler speaking at the 1936 Party rally at Nuremberg:

> That you have found me ... among so many millions is a miracle of our time! And that I have found you, that is Germany's fortune.

B Dr Otto Dietrich, Hitler's Press Secretary, writing in 1935:

> Nowhere else in the world will you find such a fanatical love of millions of people for one man, a love which is not excessive, nor ecstatic, but rather is the result of an immense and deep trust, a supreme confidence, such as children sometimes have for a very good father.

The Führer

Foreign Policy

The Treaty of Versailles was broken. Success after success was won at little cost. Hitler seemed to have made Germany great again.

Pages 32–3

The Police State

The Gestapo and SS arrested opponents of the Nazis. They were put in concentration camps and tortured. Terror kept people under control.

Pages 34–5

Propaganda

Nazi ideas were presented in a few simple slogans. All opposing views were banned.

Pages 36–9

Education

Young people joined Nazi Youth organisations. There they were taught Nazi ideas.

Pages 40–1

Economy

Jobs were created by building motorways and public buildings. The army also was made much bigger, and there were more jobs in the arms industry. Hitler had promised to end unemployment. He kept his promise.

Pages 42–5

THE IMAGE OF HITLER

C An official portrait of Hitler, painted by Heinrich Knirr in 1937. Hitler is wearing the Iron Cross he won in the First World War.

E Hitler with Eva Braun. This is a still taken from Eva Braun's home movie. The film was found after the Second World War.

The way in which Hitler was presented to the German people was an important part of the Hitler myth. Pictures of Hitler showed him as a hero. He was a real leader, a man who devoted his life to the German people. He was shown as a statesman who considered all the options and then always made the right decisions. In this way Hitler was made to appear almost god-like. However, other photographs were issued which showed Hitler as an ordinary person, a man of the people. Source B shows Hitler laughing and relaxing. Other photographs were issued showing him playing with dogs or just reading the newspaper. As Hitler toured the country the German people also got the chance to meet him. These meetings were carefully staged to create the impression that Hitler was a powerful and special man.

D Hitler laughing. This was an official photograph issued in 1935.

Q

1 a) Look at source C. What impression of Hitler does it give?
   b) Which aspects of the picture give you this impression?
2 In what way does source D give a different impression of Hitler?
3 Source E is a still taken from a home movie. The other sources were all officially produced. Why do you think that source E was not shown to the German people? The text in the 'Hitler Myth' illustration will help you to answer this question.

Foreign Policy

Key Issues | What were Hitler's foreign policy aims? Why were the armed forces increased so rapidly?

A 'One People, One Empire, One Leader'. This Nazi poster was issued in March 1938. It showed just how much Hitler had achieved in only five years.

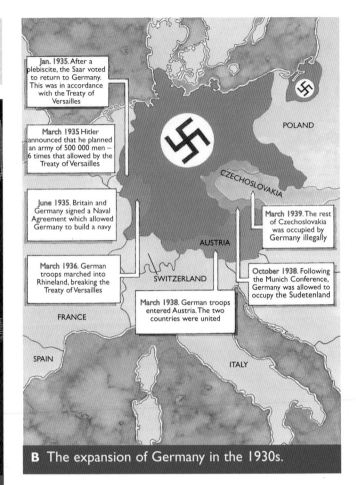

Jan. 1935. After a plebiscite, the Saar voted to return to Germany. This was in accordance with the Treaty of Versailles

March 1935 Hitler announced that he planned an army of 500 000 men – 6 times that allowed by the Treaty of Versailles

June 1935. Britain and Germany signed a Naval Agreement which allowed Germany to build a navy

March 1936. German troops marched into Rhineland, breaking the Treaty of Versailles

March 1938. German troops entered Austria. The two countries were united

March 1939. The rest of Czechoslovakia was occupied by Germany illegally

October 1938. Following the Munich Conference, Germany was allowed to occupy the Sudetenland

POLAND

CZECHOSLOVAKIA

AUSTRIA

SWITZERLAND

FRANCE

SPAIN

ITALY

B The expansion of Germany in the 1930s.

Hitler's foreign policy was vital to the Hitler myth. He was said to be a god-like leader who automatically made the right decisions. His actions in foreign policy seemed to prove that this was the case. Time and again he broke the Treaty of Versailles. He began to create a greater Germany made up of all the German-speaking people. At no time did Britain or France prevent him. He did seem always to make the right decisions. This made him very popular. Unlike previous German leaders he seemed to stand up to other countries. He achieved so much and at so little cost. No German blood was shed in achieving all these successes.

Re-armament

On 14 October 1933 Hitler took Germany out of the League of Nations. Germany would stop paying reparations. It was also a clear signal that Germany was going to ignore the limits placed on its armed forces by the Treaty of Versailles. This had limited the size of the German army to 100 000 men. It had also prevented Germany from having an airforce or from building battleships. As soon as he became Chancellor Hitler put thousands of unemployed men in the army. In 1935 he introduced **conscription**. By 1939 the German army had almost a million men. An airforce was created, known as the *Luftwaffe*. By 1939 it had over 8000 aircraft.

The Rhineland

The Treaty of Versailles had not allowed Germany to put troops in the Rhineland. In March 1936 Hitler ordered German troops into the Rhineland. The German army was not yet large enough to take on France. The German troops were under orders to retreat if the French army marched to meet them. France was not willing to act without British support and Britain refused to cooperate.

Austria

C Nazi troops march into Vienna, the capital of Austria, in 1938.

The Treaty of Versailles had banned the two major German-speaking countries of Europe, Germany and Austria, from uniting. President Wilson's principle of **self-determination** did not extend to those countries who were blamed for starting the war. Hitler was himself born in Austria. He had tried to unite the two countries in 1934, but had been stopped by the Italian leader Mussolini. By 1938 Mussolini was a close ally of Germany and so only Britain and France could prevent the union, or '*Anschluss*'. On 12 March German troops invaded Austria. Britain and France did nothing.

Czechoslovakia

The Treaty of Versailles had placed the area known as the Sudetenland in Czechoslovakia. This was in spite of the fact that it contained three million Germans. Having won in Austria Hitler believed that Britain and France would not stop him from taking over the Sudetenland. Hitler met the British Prime Minister, Neville Chamberlain, at Bad Godesberg in September 1938. Hitler demanded that the Sudetenland be given to Germany. War seemed likely. It would not be an easy war for the Germans. France had a treaty with Czechoslovakia. This promised that France would help to defend Czechoslovakia. The Czech army was almost as big as the German army and the Sudetenland contained strong defences.

The Italian dictator Mussolini suggested that Italy, Germany, France and Britain should meet to decide what should be done to prevent a war from breaking out. The meeting took place in the German city of Munich. The four countries agreed that Germany could take over the Sudetenland. In return Hitler promised that he wouldn't ask for any other areas of Europe. The Czechs were not even consulted. Chamberlain returned to Britain and claimed that he had won 'peace for our time'. Six months later German troops invaded the rest of Czechoslovakia. Hitler had won again.

D Henry Metelmann remembers how he felt about Hitler's foreign policy:

To my eyes, events were now running splendidly. The chains of Versailles were torn apart by German military occupation of the demilitarised Rhineland. Not long after that the Führer liberated his native Austria. Next, with the help of the British and French at Munich, Czechoslovakia was sold down the drain and ended up as a Protectorate of Germany. All of us youngsters were so proud and, while my parents worried about the threatening clouds of war, I believed my Hitler Youth teaching that war was a necessary cleaning process of the human race.

---

1. What were Hitler's foreign policy aims?
2. Why was Hitler able to achieve such easy success in foreign policy?
3. a) Read source D. How does it help to explain why Hitler's foreign policy made him popular with the German people?
   b) What evidence can you find to suggest that not all Germans felt this way?
   c) How do you explain this difference in attitude?
4. Hitler was sure that his policies would succeed because he believed that Britain and France would do anything to avoid a war. Does the evidence in this chapter support this view? Explain your answer.

The Police State

Key Issue **What were the powers of the police in Nazi Germany?**

Hitler wanted the German people to obey him. One way to achieve this was through propaganda (see pages 36–7). Hand in hand with this went terror. If people would not accept Nazi ideas through choice then they must be forced to accept them. Germany became a police state. This means that the police had the power to do whatever they wanted. They could decide what needed to be done 'for the good of the country'. The rights of individual German citizens counted for very little.

Hitler developed a number of organisations to enforce this terror.

A Hitler is greeted by young children as they arrive for an SS meeting in Berlin.

The SS

The SS or *Schutzstaffel* were set up in 1925 as part of the SA. In 1934 they were used to destroy the power of the SA in the Night of the Long Knives (see pages 28–9). They were led by Heinrich Himmler. They were totally loyal to Hitler and would carry out any order. They were supposed to be perfect examples of Aryan men. The SS were eventually divided into three main sections.

1 The SD or **Sicherheitdienst**. The SD were responsible for state security. That means they had to search out and deal with enemies of the Nazis.

2 The **Waffen** *SS.* These were units who fought alongside the army.

3 The Death's Head Units. These took control of the concentration camps. Originally these had been in the hands of the SA.

B Himmler describes the way of selecting recruits for the SS.

> We went about it like a seedsman who, wanting to improve the strain of a good old variety which has become crossbred and lost its vigour, goes through the fields to pick the seeds of the best plants. We sorted out the people who we thought unsuitable for the formation of the SS simply on the basis of outward appearance.

C Himmler describes the task of the SS in a lecture to army officers in 1937:

> In a future war we shall not only have the Army's front on land, the Navy's front on sea and the Airforce's front in the skies over Germany, but we shall have a fourth theatre of war: the home front! These are the grass roots which we must keep healthy by hook or by crook because otherwise the three others, the fighting parts of Germany, would once more be stabbed in the back.
>
> We must be clear about the fact that our opponent in this war is not only an opponent in a military sense, but also a political opponent ... our natural enemy, international Bolshevism, led by Jews.

The Gestapo

The Gestapo or *Geheime Staatspolizei* were the secret police. They were first set up in 1933 by Göring when he had been Prussian Minister of the Interior in Hitler's first government. In 1936 they were was given power in the whole of Germany. Like the SD their job was to search out opponents of the Nazis. The Gestapo could arrest anyone and send them to concentration camps without a trial. They used informers to uncover any attempts to organise opposition (see pages 58–9). By 1939 there were 162 000 Germans imprisoned without trial. In 1936 Himmler's deputy, Richard Heydrich, became the head of the Gestapo. This meant that the Gestapo was in effect under SS control.

D The barracks at the Dachau concentration camp.

The courts

Since the SD and the Gestapo could put people in concentration camps without a trial the courts could not protect Germans from their police. However, this was not to be the role of the courts. The judges were replaced by Nazi supporters. This meant that opponents of the Nazis would still be punished even if they did get a trial. In 1934 Hitler set up the People's Court. This was to try 'enemies of the state'. Of course any opponent of the Nazis could be called an enemy of the state. By 1939 it had sentenced over 500 people to death and sent many others to the concentration camps.

The concentration camps

Concentration camps were prisons set up for Hitler's enemies. The first of these was at Dachau. It was opened in 1933. Others soon followed. They were supposedly to 'correct' opponents so that they stopped opposing the Nazis. As sources E and F suggest they were places of torture. Many prisoners died in the concentration camps. During the war camps such as Dachau became extermination camps (see page 54)

E Regulations for Dachau concentration camp, October 1933.

Tolerance means weakness. In the light of this, punishment will be mercilessly handed out whenever the interests of the Fatherland require it. The fellow countryman who is decent but misled will never be affected by these regulations.

F Stefan Zender recounts his experience of Oranienburg concentration camp.

I and three other leaders of the Socialist Workers' Party were ordered into the punishment stockade, a wooden structure 60 cm by 60 cm. You could only stand upright in it – you couldn't sit or even bend. I was in it for four days. I was beaten repeatedly in between. After four days my whole body was swollen from standing up.

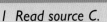

1 Read source C.
   a) What is Himmler referring to when he says that German armed forces 'would once more be stabbed in the back'?
   b) According to Himmler, who are the real enemies of the SS in a war?
2 a) What impression of the SS is given by source A?
   b) How accurate is this impression?
3 a) Explain how each of the following helped the Nazis against their opponents:
   ● SS;
   ● Gestapo;
   ● the courts;
   ● the concentration camps.
   b) If Hitler was so popular, why did he need all of these to stay in power?

Propaganda and Censorship

How did the Nazis get their ideas across to the people? In what ways did art help in this?

A Hitler, writing in Mein Kampf in 1925:

The purpose of propaganda is to convince the masses, whose slowness of understanding needs to be given time in order to absorb information: only constant repetition will finally succeed in imprinting an idea on the mind.

B Goebbels, appointed by Hitler to be responsible for propaganda, speaking about its use:

The essence of propaganda is to gather complex ideas into a single slogan and then instil this into the people as a whole.

C Robert Wistrich, writing in 1995:

Together with Goebbels, Hitler was perhaps the first twentieth century leader to see clearly the similarity between selling a commercial product and marketing a politician to the people.

Look at sources A, B and C. At the end of the twentieth century it is usual for politicians to be sold like soap powder. They produce sound-bites, short statements which will be easily remembered and will fit into news' broadcasts. Seventy years earlier Goebbels and Hitler had realised that this was the way to political success. Present the public with a few simple ideas, sum up these ideas in short slogans and repeat these slogans endlessly.

Hatred of the Jews, destruction of the Treaty of Versailles, making Germany great – these were the ideas which were put across, either in words or in images.

Words

Trying to win power

Before he became Chancellor Hitler used simple slogans to get his message across. Look at the election poster on page 14. Hitler also had the benefit of the backing of Alfred Hugenberg.

Although Hugenberg was a member of the DNVP he supported Hitler after 1929. He owned a number of newspapers and he used these to help to spread Hitler's message. Hitler also benefited from developments in the technology of microphones and loudspeakers. These allowed him to address far larger meetings than would have been possible a few years earlier. Hitler was also the first German politician to realise the importance of aircraft. Hitler criss-crossed Germany during election campaigns, speaking to crowds in all parts of Germany.

In power

Once Hitler had become Chancellor he appointed Goebbels as Reich Minister of Public Enlightenment and Propaganda. This meant that Goebbels controlled the press, radio, publishing, films and the arts. No book could be published without Goebbels' permission. He also ordered the public burning of those books which disagreed with Nazi views. Newspapers which opposed the Nazis were closed down. The remaining newspapers had to get their news and their opinions from the DNB, the Nazi news agency. The Nazi publishing company, Eher Verlag, also bought up newspapers so that by 1939 it owned 67 per cent of German newspapers.

Perhaps Goebbels' greatest success was the radio. At a time when television was not available, radio offered Hitler access to the homes of ordinary people. In his first year as Chancellor Hitler made 50 radio broadcasts. German industry produced cheap radios so that everyone could afford them. By 1939 70 per cent of German families possessed a radio. This was the highest percentage ownership in the world. The radios were designed to have a short range. Therefore they could not pick up foreign stations. This meant that Germans could not pick up alternative versions of the news. They could only hear the Nazi version. People who listened to foreign radio stations during the war could be executed.

Cinema was also used to get Nazi ideas across. The cover of this book comes from a poster advertising a film showing the SA as heroes. However, Goebbels realised that people would soon become bored if all films simply showed Nazi propaganda. So he also ordered Hollywood-style musicals and epic films to be made. These would simply make people feel happy.

Image

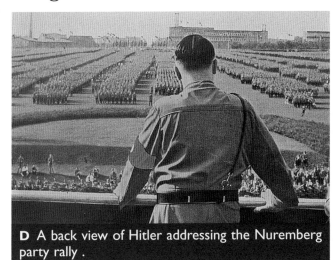

D A back view of Hitler addressing the Nuremberg party rally.

Hitler and Goebbels were well aware that there were other ways to get their message across. Image was vital. People would believe that Hitler was making Germany great if they could see it. Goebbels organised huge marches and rallies at which the SA could show off. Every year a party rally was held at Nuremberg. The sheer size and spectacle of the occasion gave the image of greatness. Perhaps the biggest single spectacle was the Berlin Olympics of 1936. A vast new stadium was built with film cameras to record the events and photo-electric timing instead of stop watches. Germany was presented as the most advanced nation. Germany also won far more medals than any other country, 'proving' the superiority of the German race.

Architecture

E Hitler's speech at the opening of the new Reich Chancellery in 1939:

> When one enters the Reich Chancellery, one should have the feeling that one is visiting the master of the world.

Image could also be provided by buildings. When he was in prison Hitler had drawn a number of sketches for new buildings for the new Germany. Once in power he put these ideas into practice with his architect Albert Speer. Borrowing the style of ancient Greece and Rome he wanted to display the greatness of the new Germany with huge public buildings. The centre of Munich became a shrine to the SA, with a temple to those who died in the 1923 Munich putsch (see pages 18–19).

Hitler also planned a massive rebuilding of Berlin. At its centre would be an Arch of Triumph, twice as high as the Arc de Triomphe in Paris. This gigantic arch would contain the names of every one of the 1.8 million Germans who had died in the First World War.

F Collect your models of Hitler and Rudolf Hess, the deputy leader of the party. Another way of getting Hitler's image into people's homes. These models date from about 1940.

G The former British Prime Minister, Lloyd George, writing in 1936:

> It is true that public criticism of the Government is forbidden in every form. That does not mean that criticism is absent. I have heard the speeches of Nazis freely condemned. But not a word of criticism or of disapproval have I heard of Hitler.

1 Read source E. What is the purpose of buildings according to Hitler?
2 Read source G.
   a) In what way does this suggest that Nazi propaganda was successful?
   b) In what way does it suggest Nazi propaganda was not successful?
3 Successful propaganda involves getting your ideas across to the people while censorship involves stopping the people learning about opposing views. Do you think that propaganda or censorship was more important to the Nazis? Explain your answer.

37
</>

ART IN NAZI GERMANY

Art before the Nazis

The early twentieth century was a period of great experimentation in art. The camera had been invented in the nineteenth century. This meant that artists were faced with a real challenge. It was no longer enough for an artist to paint what was seen. The camera could produce this much more simply. Artists had to create something different. This was perhaps best explained by the art critic and poet, Guillaume Apollinaire. He compared the role of an artist in the twentieth century with that of a composer. The sounds made by a stream, or the wind blowing through leaves in a tree may be very pleasant, but a composer does not merely copy these. The composer takes sound and constructs something totally new, which people enjoy listening to even more. Apollinaire suggested that the painter must do the same. It was not enough just to copy nature. Artists should take the images they see around them and put them together in a totally different way. The artist would therefore give people a totally new experience.

Art under the Nazis

Many people found that they could not understand modern art. It had abandoned realism. People could look at older paintings and understand what the artist was trying to express. The images were those that the eye was used to seeing. This was no longer the case with modern art. Many people hated it because they could not understand it. The Nazis exploited this hatred. They called modern art 'degenerate art'. By this they meant art which had become sick and twisted. They blamed it on Jews and other races. The art of Germany was realism.

> **Many of the artworks painted under the Nazis were captured by the Americans in 1945. They took them to America. 800 are still there.**

However the purpose of Nazi art was not simply to show things realistically. Art was propaganda. It had to show Nazi values. Each year exhibitions of German art were held. Many of the paintings illustrated the Nazi idea of 'blood and soil'. Paintings such as source D showed the simple

B *The Night*, by Max Beckman, 1919. Beckman shows a family being tortured in their own house. He is commenting on the terrible violence on the streets of Germany after the end of the First World War.

A *The Match Seller*, by Otto Dix. Dix is showing how people in the street ignore a crippled soldier from the First World War. Dix had fought throughout the war but the experience had turned him into a **pacifist**.

C Guillaume Apollinaire wrote:

The goal of painting is still what it used to be – to please the eye. The viewer henceforth has to learn to find another pleasure from the traditional pleasure that can be found in the contemplation of nature.

peasant life as ideal. This is rather ironic. The Third Reich gave the impression of being a modern society, with the greatest technological achievements. Yet it also gave the impression that the life of a peasant was the best one. It created a myth of peasant life. Everything was simple and perfect. Hard work was shown as heroic. Illness and poverty were not shown. Other Nazi pictures, such as source E, highlighted the perfect Aryan. Young German men and women were shown as having perfect bodies. They were better than other races. Nazi art had a simple message which was easy for ordinary people to understand.

The work of 'degenerate' artists like Dix was attacked. Dix himself was thrown out of the Dresden Academy of Art in 1933 and his paintings were taken from him. In 1939 he was arrested. Many other German artists decided to leave Germany. In 1937 an exhibition of 'degenerate art' was held in Munich, alongside an exhibition of German art. Two million Germans visited the 'degenerate' exhibition, three times as many as went to see the German art. This was not because most Germans liked modern art better. They went to laugh at the 'degenerate art', which was labelled in a way which made fun of the paintings.

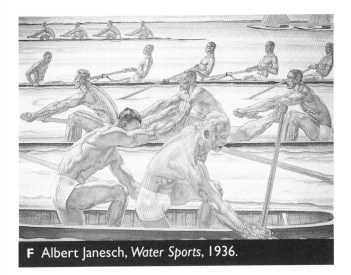

F Albert Janesch, *Water Sports*, 1936.

D Osker Martin-Amorbach, *The Sower*, 1937.

1 Look at source A. How does Dix make his point about the treatment of First World War veterans?
2 Look at source B. How does Beckman make his point about the state of Germany after the end of the war?
3 Hitler and Dix both fought throughout the First World War. They both felt that the soldiers were heroes. Why do you think that Hitler hated Dix's paintings?
4 Nazi paintings, such as sources D and F, were supposed to be a return to realistic art.
   a) In what ways were they realistic?
   b) In what ways were they not realistic?
5 How did German painting change between 1919 and 1939? What caused these changes?

14

Young People in Nazi Germany

> **A** Bernhard Rust, the Nazi Minister of Education:
>
> **The whole purpose of education is to create Nazis.**

Education

Everyone in Germany had to go to school up to the age of 14. After that schooling was optional. Boys and girls went to separate schools. All subjects were taught so that they stressed Nazi beliefs. In history, students were taught to believe that the German army had been 'stabbed in the back ' by the Weimar politicians at the end of the First World War (see source B on page 7). Biology lessons taught that Germans, as members of the Aryan race, were superior to all other races. The education of girls was concerned with turning them into perfect mothers and housewives.

> **B** A typical timetable from a girls' school. German children went to school six days a week, including Saturday.
>
> | | |
> |---|---|
> | 8.00 | German (every day) |
> | 8.50 | Geography, history or singing |
> | 9.40 | Race study or ideology (3 days each) |
> | 10.25 | Break |
> | 11.00 | Domestic science with maths (every day) |
> | 12.10 | Eugenics or health biology (3 days each) |
>
> Most afternoons would be spent in sport
> Eugenics is the study of producing perfect Aryan babies.

> **C** A German father describes a mathematics question in his son's textbook:
>
> When Klauss got back from school at five o'clock he bullied me into helping him with his homework ... Here is a maths problem picked out at random: 'A plane on take off carries 12 bombs, each weighing ten kilos. The aircraft makes for Warsaw, the centre of international Jewry. It bombs the town. On take off with all bombs on board and a fuel tank containing 1500 kilos of fuel the aircraft weighed 8 tonnes. When it returned from the crusade, there were still 230 tonnes of fuel left. What is the weight of the aircraft when empty?'

The Hitler Youth

> **D** 'Join Us! Be a part of Hitler Youth.' A poster encouraging young people to join the Hitler Youth in 1933.

The Nazis not only wanted to control what went on in schools. They set up youth organisations to control the life of young people outside school as well. Boys could join the Hitler Youth at 14, or before that its younger section the German Young People. In 1936 membership was made compulsory. Camping and hiking were popular activities. Most activities were designed to create fit young people who would make good soldiers.

> **E** Hitler speaking at the Nuremberg Party rally in September 1934:
>
> There were times ... when the ideal young man was the chap who could hold his beer and was good for a drink. But now his day is past and we like to see not the man who can hold his drink, but the young man who can stand all weathers – the hardened man. Because what matters is not how many glasses of beer he can drink, but how many punches he can stand.

The BDM

The BDM or *Bund Deutsche Mädel* (League of German Girls) was the girls' version of the Hitler Youth. It also organised camping and hiking, but to make girls fit enough to be strong mothers. Although it was the intention of the BDM to reinforce the role of the woman as housewife and mother, this may not always have been its effect. In small towns and villages girls had always led very sheltered lives, with marriage and family life the only aim. The BDM took them out of their villages for the first time, and allowed them to take part in activities that had previously been only for boys. It opened up the eyes of some girls to new horizons.

G A Nazi poster. 'Join the youth groups of the Nazi women's leagues.'

Gangs

The Nazi youth organisations were certainly popular with some young people. By 1935 over 2.3 million boys had joined the Hitler Youth and 1.5 million girls were members of the BDM. However, in the late 1930s there were signs that some young people rejected the Nazi way. Gangs began to appear on street corners. They were mainly made up of 14–17 year olds. This was because most gang members had left school at 14 and at 18 they would be conscripted into the Reich Labour Service or the armed forces. The gangs were a reaction against the way the Nazis tried to organise every aspect of young people's lives. Like the Hitler Youth they would go hiking and camping, but they were not supervised by adults. They played their own music and boys and girls were free to be together. In contrast, the Hitler Youth and BDM camps were strictly single sex. Many gangs went looking for the Hitler Youth and beat them up. Some gangs considered themselves to be part of a larger movement, the 'Edelweiss Pirates'. They wore a metal badge of the edelweiss flower. They were not only concerned with having fun, but also became anti-Nazi rather than just anti-authority, especially once the war had started (see page 58).

1 Why do you think that the Nazis set up the Hitler Youth?
2 Camps and hikes took young people away from their parents. Why do you think the Nazis wanted to do this?
3 Source A says that the purpose of education was to create Nazis. Do you think it succeeded? Use the sources and the evidence from the text to back up your answer.

15

The Economy Under the Nazis

How did Hitler deal with the problem of unemployment? Was Hitler able to make Germany economically self-sufficient?

Unemployment

In the 1930s there was an economic depression throughout most of the world. The high unemployment it created was an important reason why the Nazis came to power. In his election campaigns Hitler promised to provide 'bread and work' for the German people. This was a promise he could not afford to break. Millions of ordinary Germans needed a job. They would worship a political leader who could cure unemployment. Just as he did with his foreign policy, Hitler would be able to portray himself as a hero who was rescuing the German people from a period of national humiliation. Curing unemployment was a crucial building block in the Hitler myth.

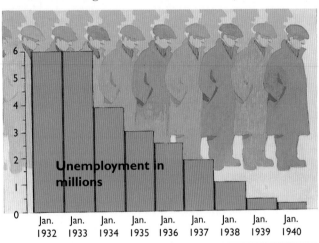

A German unemployment figures (above) compared with British unemployment figures (below).

Look at source A. Hitler was far more successful than the British government during the same period. How was Hitler able to achieve such a dramatic fall in German unemployment? There were four main reasons:

1 Reparations. Hitler stopped paying reparations once he had come to power. This meant that money which had been going to France and Belgium could now be invested in the German economy and so create more jobs. How was this money spent?

2 Government spending. Hitler sought to create jobs through government spending on construction. Germany built a network of motorways, known as *autobahns*, across the country. The *autobahns* not only created jobs. Once built they helped make German industry more efficient by increasing the speed at which goods could cross the country. Of course they also increased the speed at which troops could cross the country.

As well as the *autobahns*, huge public buildings were constructed. The Olympic Games in 1936 were held at the newly built Olympic Stadium in Berlin. Such buildings not only created jobs but also impressed people. They were a visible sign that Hitler was making Germany great again.

The Reich Labour Service was set up. This not only provided men to build the *autobahns*, but was also involved in many other projects. For instance, it drained marshes so that they could be used for farmland. It also built sea walls to protect coastal areas from flooding.

The government also invested money in the car industry. This produced the Volkswagen, the people's car. An expanded German car industry created jobs by cutting the imports of foreign cars. Car factories were also useful as they could quickly switch production to military needs.

3 Wage and price controls. Hitler had promised jobs but he also destroyed the power of the trade unions. Wages were then kept low. This was a reward for the industrialists who supported Hitler. It helped them to make big profits. This made sure that industrialists would want Hitler to stay in power.

4 Rearmament. This was only really significant after 1936. Before this Hitler concentrated on providing the bread and work which he had promised. From 1936 onwards Hitler changed the aims of the

B Hitler used buildings to show how great Germany was. For instance, if this dome had been built, it would have been the biggest in the world and would have held 180 000 people.

economy. The drive for rearmament created still more jobs and so unemployment fell still further. It was not simply that more money was spent on building weapons. Far more men were recruited into the army. When Hitler came to power the army was limited to just 100 000 men by the Treaty of Versailles. By 1938 the figure had risen to 900 000 men.

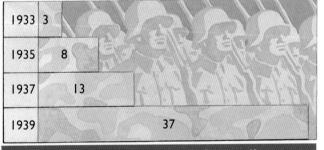

1933	3
1935	8
1937	13
1939	37

D Expenditure on the armed forces (figures in millions of marks).

C Hitler is presented with a Volkswagen by the car's inventor, Dr Ferdinand Porsche. It was a birthday present. The SS leader Himmler is sitting behind Hitler.

Q

1 Look at source A.
   a) Which country had the greater unemployment in 1932?
   b) Which country had the greater unemployment in 1938?
2 Look at source D. How does this source help to explain why Hitler was successful in reducing unemployment?
3 'Breaking the Treaty of Versailles was crucial to Germany's economic success.' Do you agree with this interpretation? Use the sources and information in the text to support your argument.

AUTARKY

What was autarky?

A Hitler, writing in 1936:

It is impossible for us, at present, to manufacture certain raw materials which we lack in Germany. The final solution lies in extending our living space, that is to say, extending the sources of raw materials and foodstuffs for our people.

Bread and work were not Hitler's only aims. He also wanted to establish **autarky**, that is make Germany economically self-sufficient. This meant Hitler wanted to stop Germany being dependent on imports, especially **raw materials**. Hitler feared that Germany would not be able to depend on imported raw materials once war had begun. However, Hitler also wanted to build up the German armed forces, and this required huge quantities of raw materials. Therefore the army would have to invade the east and capture *Lebensraum* or 'living space'. This living space would add to the production of Germany's raw materials.

B 'Help Hitler build. Buy German goods.' A Nazi poster encouraging Germans to help in the struggle to achieve autarky.

The economy under Schacht

In 1934 Hjalmar Schacht was made Economics Minister. He was not a Nazi. In Weimar Germany he had been the head of the *Reichsbank* and he had played an important role in negotiating the Dawes and Young plans.

He aimed to improve Germany's level of raw materials by making trade deals with less developed countries. These countries would be paid in German manufactured goods. He also gave priority to those raw materials which were vital to rearmament. Imports of cotton and wool were cut while imports of iron ore increased. Schacht's policies certainly enabled Germany to pay for rearmament and encouraged the growth of German industry. However, they made Germany more dependent on imported raw materials, not less.

The economy under Göring

C 'Hurrah, the butter is finished.' This was produced by the German artist John Heartfield. His real name was Helmut Herzfeld but he changed it as a protest against the Nazis.

D The German historian, Detlev Peukert, writing in 1982:

In order to keep up the feeling of success and the hopes of recovery the National Socialists were even prepared ... to import materials for consumer goods as well as products and raw materials needed for rearmament. Despite their pleas for 'guns not butter', the Nazis knew, so to speak, which side their bread was really buttered.

Schacht resigned as Economics Minister in 1937. The year before, Göring had drawn up a Four Year Plan for the economy. This set much higher targets for rearmament. It also wanted to make sure that Germany moved much closer to achieving autarky. Göring said, 'In the decisive hour it would not be a question of how much butter Germany has but how many guns'.

Experiments were begun to try and produce artificial replacements for vital raw materials that could only be obtained from abroad. Modern armed forces were dependent upon oil. So the chemical company IG Farben were paid to try to develop a method of extracting oil from coal. Attempts were also made to develop an artificial rubber. Although these experiments did create jobs they did not reduce the amount of goods which Germany imported

Agriculture

Farmers had been important supporters of the Nazis in the late 1920s and early 1930s. Hitler's food minister Darre sought to reward German farmers and protect them from the effects of the Depression. He cut the taxes that farmers had to pay and also ordered them to reduce the amount of land under cultivation. This cut food over-production and so caused food prices to rise. This was good for the farmers. However, it also meant that more food had to be imported and so did not help to create autarky.

E Gregor Strasser, a leading Nazi, speaking to the Reichstag:

Germany is still dependent on foreign countries for the most important human need: namely foodstuffs ... We must enable sufficient essential foodstuffs to be produced on German soil to feed our whole population.

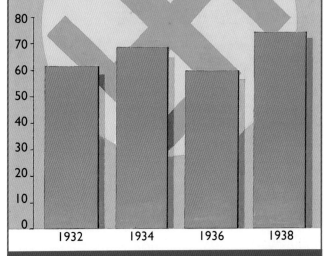

These import figures represent a comparison with German trade in 1913, before the First World War. The figures for 1913 are given a value of 100. So a figure of 50 in the import column would mean that Germany was importing half as much produce as had been the case in 1913.

F German imports.

G Schacht's opinion of Göring written in 1949:

Göring set out, with all the folly and incompetence of the amateur, to carry out the programme of economic self-sufficiency, or autarky, envisaged in the Four Year Plan.

1 a) Why did Hitler want to achieve autarky?
 b) Look at source A. What did Hitler believe needed to happen for Germany to achieve autarky?
 c) Look back to pages 42–43. How far had this been achieved by 1938?
2 a) Look at source C. What Nazi slogan is Heartfield referring to in his title 'Hurrah, the butter is finished'?
 b) What point is Heartfield making about the German economy?
 c) Does source D agree with source C?
 d) Does source F support the view given in source D?
3 Do you believe that Germany was becoming self-sufficient by 1938? Use the sources in this unit and your own knowledge to back up your answer.

16

Workers in Nazi Germany

Reich Labour Service

If the Nazis were going to win the support of workers they needed to provide jobs and improve living standards. The Reich Labour Service was set up for all school leavers and unskilled workers. They carried out projects which required large numbers of unskilled workers, such as draining marshes. (See page 42.)

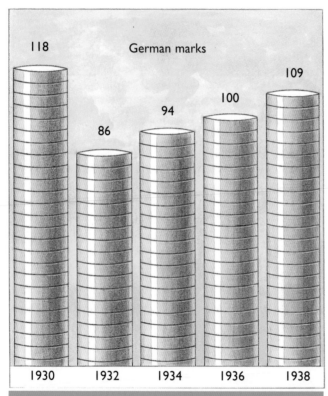

A Average weekly wages. The wages for 1936 are taken as the figure 100. If wages increase by five per cent then this would be shown as 105.

The German Labour Front

The German Labour Front was set up to replace trade unions. Trade unions had been too closely connected to the socialist and communist parties, the enemies of the Nazis. In their place the Nazis put the concept of '*Volkgemeinschaft*'. This was the idea of everyone working together for the good of the country. The Nazis wanted people to return to the spirit of the First World War, when everyone had been prepared to sacrifice themselves for the good of the country. So the German Labour Front was set up. It had complete control of all industrial workers. It set the levels of pay and the hours of work.

German Labour Front committees contained representatives of the employers as well as workers. The committees could only recommend higher wages or better working conditions. Their recommendations did not have to be acted upon. The needs of the employers were more important than the needs of the workers. The members of the committees were elected. In 1934 and 1935 this led to many opponents of the Nazis being elected. So the Nazis abandoned elections. They did not want to give their opponents a chance to express their views.

German unemployment certainly fell. German workers also looked for better working conditions. The problem was that employers did not want to pay the extra money this would cost. The workers also had to pay to belong to the Nazi organisations. The contributions were higher than they used to pay to belong to trade unions. Therefore they expected some benefits. Two organisations, the SdA and the KdF, were set up to achieve this.

Schönheit der Arbeit (SdA)

SdA or 'Beauty of Labour' was a branch of the German Labour Front. Its job was to improve conditions in the workplace. This might involve improving the safety of machines or reducing the levels of noise in a factory. However, German workers had to work much harder under the Nazis. By 1939 the average person worked a 49-hour week. By 1945 the needs of the war meant that the average working week had increased to 60 hours. Wages did not increase nearly as much as working hours. *Volkgemeinschaft* had its price.

B Robert Ley, the head of the German Labour Front, commented:

> **Today ... the worker enjoys the magnificent achievements of German drama and German music, the best German orchestras, the best German opera and theatre performances and the best German film ... Whoever works hard should be able to enjoy himself thoroughly, so that his value to the nation increases.**

C A German Labour Front poster offering workers KdF cruises in 1938

E 'The worker in the empire of the swastika.' A SPD election poster from before the time that Hitler became Chancellor.

Kraft durch Freude

KdF or 'Strength through Joy' was another branch of the German Labour Front. It was set up to provide workers with activities when they were not working. German workers were going to have to work much harder. So KdF would reward them. Those who worked hardest could be rewarded with a cruise on a KdF ship. In fact very few workers ever managed this. For the majority it was cheap concerts and theatre visits. KdF also led to the Volkswagen, the people's car. However, few Germans received a car of their own.

D A secret report by the illegal SPD on the effect of the KdF:

KdF events have become very popular ... KdF is now running weekly theatre trips into Munich from the countryside. Special trains are coming to Munich on weekdays from as far away as 120 km. It has therefore been made easy for people from the countryside to go to the theatre in the city. These trips are very popular.

1 Read source B.
   a) Apart from 'the' what is the commonest word which Ley uses?
   b) What does this tell you about the Nazis?
   c) According to Ley, what is the purpose of the KdF?
2 Does source D suggest that the KdF was successful? Do you think that source D is a reliable source on the KdF?

Extended writing

Look at source E.
a) What point is it making about the way that the Nazis will treat the workers?
b) Was the SPD right?
To answer this question you will need to look at a number of areas and decide whether or not the workers benefited. For instance, you should look at:

● unemployment;
● the abolition of trade unions;
● working conditions;
● wages;
● KdF.

Different, not Inferior – Women in Nazi Germany

How did Nazi rule affect the life of women?

A Adolf Wissel, *Farm family from Kahlenberg, 1939.*

B The Nazi, Gottfried Feder, on the role of women:

> The Jews have stolen the woman from us ... we must kill the dragon to restore her to her holy position as servant and maid.

The role of women

The Nazis believed that the place for a woman was in the home. Nazi paintings and posters showed the role of women as having children and looking after their husbands. Girls were taught this in school (see page 40). Girls were also told not to smoke or diet. It was felt that both smoking and dieting could affect their ability to have healthy children.

Professional women, such as doctors and lawyers, were forced to give up their jobs and produce children. Many teachers also gave up their jobs. However, the Nazis felt that since women had a special role in bringing up young children, it was suitable for them to teach young children in schools. Nazi propaganda showed the family as the centre of life in Germany, and women were the centre of family life. While they stayed at home it was the role of men to earn money to keep the family. Nazi slogans described the role of women as 'Different, not inferior'.

C Mother and child, a Nazi poster which was part of a campaign to encourage women to have more children.

D Hitler speaking in 1935 about the role of women:

> The woman has her own battlefield. With every child that she brings into the world, she fights the battle for the nation.

Women and children

Producing children was vital for the Nazis. They saw children as the first generation who would grow up in a Nazi world. They would accept Nazi beliefs and firmly establish Nazi rule in Germany. However, when Hitler came to power the birth rate had fallen from two million births a year in 1900 to less than one million. This was hardly surprising. The First World War had led to a shortage of men, so that 1.8 million German women were unmarried. The Nazis therefore introduced a number of laws to encourage women to have more children. Marriage loans of 600 marks were given to women who gave up work in order to get married. These loans did not have to be paid back if the woman had at least four children.

Women were also awarded an Honour Cross for having children, with a gold award for those who had eight. It was awarded on 12 August each year, Hitler's mother's birthday. In 1939 three million women received a medal for having produced four or more children. The birth rate did rise. There were 970 000 babies born in Germany in 1933. This had risen to 1 413 000 by 1939. Anti-abortion laws were also enforced and contraceptives were hard to get. There was another side to these laws. The Nazis only wanted healthy Aryan children to be born. So Jews could not have marriage loans. Any woman thought to have a hereditary disease could be sterilised. By 1945 over 300 000 men and women in Germany had been sterilised.

The effects of Nazi policies

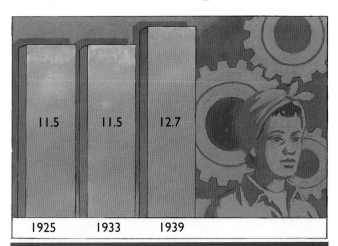

11.5 11.5 12.7

1925 1933 1939

E Women in employment (figures in millions).

As source E shows, there were more women working after six years of Nazi rule than there had been at the start. Why was this?

By 1939 the economy was set up for war. Large numbers of workers were needed in industry and there were no longer long queues of unemployed men waiting for a job. The Nazis needed women to work in the factories. This became even more vital once war had broken out. So many men were needed to fight, and as the casualties mounted women had to take on the role of wage earner and mother. However, the Nazis never did introduce conscription for women. Unlike the situation in Britain, women were not forced to work or join the armed forces.

Other Nazi policies did not always produce all of the desired effects. The League of German Girls, the BDM, was set up to educate girls in family life and to make them healthy so that they could produce lots of children. In the countryside this had always been the role of women. Girls grew up expecting to be housewives. But the BDM took them away from their families when they went on camps and hikes. By taking them away from the control of their parents it offered them new experiences. The KdF, Strength through Joy, also offered ordinary German families new opportunities and experiences. The radio, which the Nazis encouraged everyone to buy, had a similar effect. People became more aware of life outside their own town or village.

F The effect of the BDM, according to the historian Richard Grunberger:

The degree of parental control naturally was less as young people went to camp and hostels for long periods at a time. In 1936, when approximately 100 000 members of the Hitler Youth and the BDM attended the Nuremberg Rally, 900 girls between 15 and 18 returned home pregnant.

G The American, William Shirer, on the effect of the BDM:

Moral problems also arose during the Household Year for girls, in which half a million BDM girls spent a year at domestic service in a city home. Actually, the more sincere Nazis did not consider them moral problems at all. On more than one occasion I listened to women leaders of the BDM lecture their young charges on the moral and patriotic duty of bearing children for Hitler's Reich – within marriage if possible, but without it if necessary.

1 What image of women is shown in source A?
2 Why did the Nazis encourage this attitude towards women?
3 Hitler wanted women to stay at home and bring up their children. After six years of Nazi rule there were more women in work than in 1933. Does this mean that Hitler's policies had failed? Explain your answer.
4 The Nazis claimed that their policies treated women as 'different but not inferior'. Do the sources and text support this claim?

The German churches

When the Nazis came to power in Germany in 1933 most Germans were Christians.
They belonged to one of two churches. The Catholic Church was a united church which was based in Rome. The Pope was the head of the Catholic Church. The Catholic Church was very strong in southern Germany, especially in the Nazis' home state of Bavaria. There was also a group of German churches who were collectively called the Protestant churches. They had no single head. Many of the Protestant churches openly supported the Nazis. At first the Catholic Church did so as well. In 1933 Hitler signed the Concordat with the Pope. This agreement said that the Catholic Church would be left alone by the Nazis provided the Church stayed out of politics.

Why did the churches support the Nazis?

Since the Nazis were such a violent organisation it might seem surprising that the Christian churches were willing to support them. There were three reasons why this happened:

● To many Christians, Weimar Germany seemed to be a very immoral country. By contrast the Nazis supported the family and old-fashioned moral standards.

● Hitler tried to win over Christians by expressing his support for the church in his speeches.

● Most important of all was the Nazis' opposition to communism. Communists wanted to destroy Christianity and so the church feared them. Hitler seemed to many Germans to be the only hope in the struggle against communism.

The growing struggle

The Catholic Church soon discovered that they could not trust the Nazis – they were not left alone. The Catholic Church had a well-supported youth organisation. This was in direct competition with the Hitler Youth. Many Catholic parents preferred to send their children to the Catholic Youth than to the Hitler Youth. In 1937 the Catholic Youth was made illegal. The Catholic Church also ran a large number of schools. Children educated in these schools were not subjected to the level of propaganda faced by children in schools run by the state. From the Nazi viewpoint this might lead to these children growing up as opponents of Nazis. At first the schools were made to remove Christian symbols, such as the crucifix, from classrooms. Later the schools were taken out of church control. Many teachers and parents opposed this. In 1937 the Pope protested to Hitler.

It has been estimated that as many as one third of all Catholic priests were punished by the Nazis. At least 400 were put in a special block at Dachau concentration camp. Catholic churches were packed every Sunday. Church leaders were often applauded by the people when they appeared in

A The *Reichsbishop* arranges Christianity. A poster by the Communist John Heartfield (see page 44).

B Another poster by Heartfield. Christ is shown accepting the help of the Nazis in repairing the cross.

D Bishop Meiser, the head of the Protestant Church in Bavaria, praying in 1937:

> We thank You, Lord, for every success which, through Your grace, You have granted to Hitler for the good of the people.

One of their leaders was Pastor Martin Niemöller. He was arrested by the Nazis and spent seven years in Sachsenhausen and Dachau concentration camps. Another leader was Dietrich Bonhoeffer. During the war he tried to organise resistance to the Nazis. He was even in contact with the Allies. In 1943 he was also imprisoned in a concentration camp. In 1945 he was murdered by the Gestapo. This was the problem faced by any churchman who tried to oppose the Nazis. Anything that they wrote or said was noted by the Gestapo. They had the choice of either staying quiet or being silenced. Most chose to support Hitler even if they complained about local Nazis.

The propaganda of the Hitler myth certainly worked. Hitler was seen as the saviour of Germany. It was his supporters, and not the *Führer* himself, who were seen as attacking the churches.

Nazi religion

The Nazis even set up their own Christian church so that they could gain control of Christianity. Although some Protestants did support the new church it was not a great success.

A further attempt to remove the influence of the Christian churches was the Faith Movement. The Nazis set up a pagan, that is non-Christian, religion. This fitted in well with many Nazi ideas. In stressing that the Aryan race was superior, they used Nordic myths to appeal to feelings of past greatness. These myths were pagan.

public. However, the Catholic Church rarely publicly opposed the Nazi government. To do so would have led to severe punishment. For instance, the church leaders did not protest about the attacks on the Jews on Kristallnacht (see page 53).

The Protestants were divided. Many Protestants continued to support the Nazis. Bishop Meiser (Source D) was one example. However, other Protestants opposed Hitler. One such group was called the Confessing Church.

In 1941 one Catholic Church leader, Cardinal Galen, did openly criticise the Nazis for killing mentally ill people. He ended the war in Sachsenhausen Concentration Camp.

C A Protestant pastor speaking about his attitude to the Nazis in 1937:

> We all know that if the Third Reich were to collapse today, communism would come in its place. Therefore we must show loyalty to our *Führer*, who has saved us from Communism and given us a better future.

1 Look at sources A and B.
   a) In source A, in what way has the bishop organised the German church?
   b) In source B, what is the SA man doing to the cross?
   c) What is the artist suggesting about the attitude of the German churches towards the Nazis?
2 Do you think that the churches were right to try and cooperate with the Nazis? Explain your answer using evidence from these pages.

19

The Treatment of the Jews

Key Issues

How did the Nazis treat the Jews? What was the 'Final Solution' and why did the Nazis want to carry it out?

On page 16 you will have noted that anti-Semitism was an important Nazi belief, although the Nazis weren't the only ones to believe in it. However, the Nazis took their hatred of the Jews to a terrible level. They blamed the Jews for most of Germany's problems.

The Jews were an easy target. In 1933 Jews made up just one per cent of the German population. However, they did make up 16 per cent of all lawyers and 10 per cent of all doctors. Many Germans were jealous of their success and suspicious of their different religion.
As soon as Hitler became Chancellor of Germany life became more difficult for Jews. As early as March 1933 Hitler ordered the SA to turn customers away from Jewish shops. They also smashed up some windows in Jewish shops. People were ordered to stop using Jewish lawyers, and Jewish doctors and nurses were ordered to attend only Jewish patients. Things soon got much worse.

B An excerpt from a Nazi schoolbook:

Inge sits in the doctor's waiting room ... Again and again her mind dwells on the warnings of the BDM leader: 'A German must not consult a Jew doctor! And particularly not a German girl! Many a girl who has gone to a Jew doctor to be cured has found disease and disgrace'.

The door opens. Inge looks in. There stands the Jew. She screams. She's so frightened she drops the magazine. She jumps up in terror. Her eyes stare into the Jewish doctor's face. His face is the face of the devil. In the middle of the devil's face is a huge crooked nose. Behind the spectacles two criminal eyes. And thick lips that are grinning. A grin that says: 'Now I've got you at last, little German girl.'

In 1935 the Nuremberg Laws were passed. These made it illegal for Jews to marry non-Jews, or even to have sexual intercourse with them. Jews were deprived of German citizenship and so lost the right to vote. Jews were also stopped from using swimming pools, restaurants and other public facilities. Jews were defined as anyone who had at

A Anti-Semitic cartoon from a Nazi children's book of 1938. The Jews, both adult and children, are shown with very dark hair and big noses.

least one Jewish grandparent. In schools children were taught to hate Jews. It is hardly surprising that between 1933 and 1938 30 per cent of all Jews emigrated from Germany.

C The Jewish lawyer, Michael Siegal, is forced to wear a placard which says 'I am a Jew, I will never again complain about the Nazis.' It is March 1933. He had tried to complain to the police about Nazi behaviour in smashing a neighbour's shop window.

D A member of the SA stands outside a Jewish shop in 1933. The sign reads 'Germans! Beware! Do not buy from Jewish shops'.

Kristallnacht

In 1938 a German diplomat in Paris was shot dead by Herschel Grynszpan. Grynszpan had heard that 17 000 Jews, including his own family, had been deported from Germany but left stranded on the border with Poland when the Poles refused to accept them. The German response to the murder was to launch an attack on Jews and Jewish property on the night of 9 November. This became known as *Kristallnacht*, a reference to all the broken glass resulting from the destruction. 7500 Jewish businesses were destroyed and over 30 000 Jews were sent to concentration camps.

E The *Daily Telegraph*, 12 November 1938. An eyewitness account of *Kristallnacht*:

Mob law ruled in Berlin throughout this afternoon and evening, and hordes of hooligans indulged in an orgy of destruction. I have seen several anti-Jewish outbreaks during the last five years, but never anything as sickening as this.

Racial hatred and hysteria seemed to have taken complete hold of otherwise decent people. I saw fashionably dressed women clapping their hands and screaming with glee, while respectable mothers held up their babies to see the 'fun'.

The fashionable shopping centre of the capital has been reduced to a shambles, with the streets littered with the wreckage of sacked Jewish shops and offices. No attempt was made by the police to stop the rioters.

The attacks on Jews and their property started all over Germany, as if by a signal, soon after midnight, when the beer-halls closed … The caretaker of the synagogue in the Prinzregentenstrasse is reported to have been burnt to death together with his family. It is learned on good authority that two Jews were lynched in Berlin's East End early this morning and two more in the West End.

1 How does source B show the Jews in an unfavourable way?
2 In what way does source A give a similar image of Jews to that in source B?
3 What evidence can you find in source E to suggest that Kristallnacht was centrally organised?

THE FINAL SOLUTION

Once the Second World War had begun the situation got much worse. As the German army conquered Poland it brought another three million Jews under Nazi control. The decision was taken to introduce the 'Final Solution'. All Jews in the areas of Europe controlled by the Nazis were to be exterminated. Between 1942 and 1945 six million Jews perished in extermination camps such as Auschwitz and Sobibor – an event known as the Holocaust. This was the work of the SS.

A Rivka Yosselevska, who survived a Nazi mass murder of Jews, describes what she saw:

We turned towards the grave and then he [an SS soldier] turned around and asked, 'Whom shall I shoot first?' We were already facing the grave. The German asked, 'Whom do you want me to shoot first?' I did not answer. I felt him take the child from my arms. The child cried out and was shot immediately. And then he aimed at me. First he held on to my hair and turned my head around; I stayed standing; I heard a shot, but I continued to stand and he turned my head again and he aimed the revolver at me, ordered me to watch, and then turned my head around and shot at me. Then I fell to the ground into the pit amongst the bodies, but I felt nothing.

B Jews in Warsaw are rounded up to be taken the the extermination camps in 1943. The young boy in the centre of the photograph managed to survive the war.

At first Jews were rounded up and shot. Source A describes such an event. However, the Germans needed to kill more Jews than they could by just shooting them. Gas chambers were built which could kill 2000 Jews at a time. Their bodies were then burnt. Jews were taken to the extermination camps by train. Since no one left the camps the new arrivals had no idea what to expect. On arrival they were divided into two groups. Those who were young and fit were put to work. The others went to the gas chambers. The survivors were no better off. They were worked to death in the labour camps.

Why did the Nazis carry out the Final Solution?

We cannot be sure why the mass murder of the Jews took place. Hitler was certainly obsessed with hatred for the Jews. He blamed them for Germany's defeat in the First World War. He also blamed them for starting the Second World War. However, he had not tried to wipe them out before 1941. This might be because Jews made up fewer than one per cent of the German population. Once Germany had conquered Poland and part of the Soviet Union they had far more Jews under their control. Perhaps it was now possible to destroy most Jews. Perhaps there were simply too many to keep alive in concentration camps. However source D would seem to suggest that Hitler intended to kill them all along.

C Alfons Hock, a member of the Hitler Youth, interviewed in 1989:

It would be fair to point out that I myself never met even the most fanatic Nazi who wanted the extermination of the Jews. Certainly we wanted the Jews out of Germany, but we did not want them to be killed.

D Hitler, speaking to the Reichstag on 30 January 1939:

If the international Jewish financiers in and outside Europe should succeed in plunging the nations once more into world war, then the result will be ... the annihilation of the Jewish race in Europe.

E A painting of the scene which greeted the British troops who arrived at the Belsen concentration camp. The painting is by Leslie Cole.

F Höss, the commandant of Auschwitz, describes how he felt after killing one million Jews. He is speaking after the war was over.

I had to watch coldly while mothers with laughing children went to the gas chamber. I had to see everything. I had to watch hour by hour, by night and by day, the burning and the removal of the bodies, the extraction of the teeth, the cutting of the hair, the whole grisly business ... I had to do all this, because I was the one to whom everyone looked, because I had to show them all that I did not merely issue orders and make regulations but was also prepared to be present at whatever task ... In the face of such grim considerations I was forced to bury all human feelings as deeply as possible.

G A speech by Himmler to SS leaders in October 1943:

'The Jewish people will be exterminated,' says every party comrade, 'it's clear, it's in our programme. Elimination of the Jews, extermination, and we'll do it.' And then they come along, the worthy eighty million Germans, and each one of them produces his decent Jew. It's clear the others are swine, but this one is a fine Jew. Not one of those who talk like that has watched it happening, not one of them has been through it. Most of you will know what it means when a hundred corpses are lying side by side, or five hundred or a thousand are lying there ... We have exterminated a bacterium because we do not want to be infected by the bacterium and die of it.

The end of anti-Semitism?

Anti-Semitism was not unique to the Nazis. It still exists today. Even in Germany. At the end of the twentieth century the SS guards who watched over the Jewish slave labourers at Auschwitz receive a pension from the German government. When the war ended some of the German Jews in Auschwitz's slave labour camp were still alive. They don't get a pension. The German government says that this is because none of them paid any insurance contributions during the war!

1 a) What do sources C and G tell you about the attitude of ordinary Germans to the murder of the Jews?
   b) In what way do sources F and G give a different impression of the opinion of Nazis about the murder of the Jews?
   c) What reasons can you think of to explain this difference?
2 After the war many Germans claimed that they couldn't be blamed for the Holocaust because they didn't know what was happening to the Jews. Do you think that:
   a) this was likely?
   b) only leading Nazis can be blamed for these crimes?
Using these sources and your own knowledge explain whether you agree or disagree with points (a) and (b).

20

Treatment of the Minorities

Key Issue

Why were minority groups targeted by the Nazis?

A *The Brown Shirts Take Over*, by Elk Eber. This shows men as the Aryan ideal; blond, strong and loyal.

B 'Healthy and unhealthy genetic stock.' These illustrations come from a 1943 secondary school biology textbook.

Between 1933 and 1939 the Nazis treated the Jews as *untermensch*. They were second class human beings. They were not the only Germans to be treated in this way. Other groups also found themselves treated badly by the Nazis.

The gypsies

The gypsies were unpopular with many Germans before Hitler came to power. However, the Nazis took this to new levels. They targeted the gypsies for two reasons.

1 They were 'aliens'. In other words they were not Aryans. They were not part of the superior German race.
2 They were 'asocial'. They did not settle in one area and did not have regular jobs. This meant they could not be part of the *Volkgemeinschaft*, the idea of self-sacrifice that the Nazis wanted to instil in all Germans. (See page 46.)

C Dr Robert Ritter, head of the Nazi Institute of Criminal Biology.

The gypsy question can be considered solved only when the majority of the asocial and unproductive gypsies are placed in large work camps and the further reproduction of this half-caste population is terminated.

Nazi scientists regarded gypsies as inferior by race. Therefore gypsies could never be taught how to be good Germans. In 1935 they were classified as 'aliens' and so were subject to the Nuremberg Laws, along with the Jews. In October 1939 all gypsies were ordered to be sent to concentration camps in the newly conquered Poland. In 1940 2500 gypsies were deported. In 1942 all gypsies were taken to a special gypsy camp which was part of the Auschwitz-Birkenau concentration camp in Poland. Unlike the Jews the gypsies were not put in gas chambers. However 20 000 of them were sent to Auschwitz. In 1944 the Russian army was advancing towards the camp. The SS shot all the gypsies before leaving. In total it is thought that the Nazis murdered over 200 000 of Europe's gypsies.

Vagrants

Gypsies and Jews were not the only 'asocials' in Germany according to the Nazis. There were also vagrants. Various groups made up vagrants. They might be men moving from town to town seeking work. They might be young people who had left home. They might be beggars. The Nazi solution was to force these people to work. In 1938 the SS reported that they had gathered up more than 10 000 vagrants and put them in concentration camps. There the vagrants were being 'educated' in how to work.

D Hilde Eisenhardt, head of the German Association for Public and Private Welfare, speaking in 1938:

We need their hands to help us in the great economic programme that lies ahead, and therefore cannot continue to allow people who are capable of work to spend months and years on the open roads.

E Himmler, the head of the SS, describing why vagrants should be put in work education camps:

Vagrants are to be made to do very hard work, so that they can be forcibly brought to realise that their behaviour is bad for the nation, so that they can be trained to work in an orderly and regulated fashion.

F 'Degenerate Music.' This is the cover of a guidebook to an exhibition in 1938. Note that the physical features of the black musician are exaggerated. The star shown on his lapel is the Star of David – the sign of the Jews.

The black American athlete, Jesse Owens, won four gold medals at the Nazi-organised Berlin Olympics of 1936. Hitler was furious!

Black people

Although there were few black people in Germany they were also subject to the Nuremberg Laws. Germans were not allowed to marry them. In the 1920s black American music had been very popular. The Nazis regarded this as 'degenerate' and un-German. They treated black people in a similar way to the gypsies. They sterilised any children who were born to German women by black soldiers who had been stationed in the Rhineland after the First World War.

Mentally ill

The Nazis considered mental illness to be hereditary and so incurable. The Nazis sterilised those people they considered to be mentally ill. By 1945 they had sterilised up to 300 000 people. Once the war had begun it was decided that the mentally ill were of no use and so should be killed. The so-called 'Public Ambulance Service Ltd' was set up. By August 1941 it had murdered 70 000 mentally ill people.

Homosexuals

The Weimar republic had allowed homosexuals some freedom. Source E on page 13 describes a gay club. Despite the fact that some leading Nazis, such as Röhm, were homosexual, the Nazis made homosexuality illegal. The role of adults was to produce babies and homosexuals would not carry out this role. In 1943 Himmler ordered the death penalty for all homosexuals found in the SS and police.

1 Look at source F. What were the Nazis suggesting by putting the Star of David on a black person?
2 Why did the Nazis consider gypsies and vagrants to be asocial?
3 In what ways were vagrants treated differently from gypsies?
4 Explain why vagrants were treated differently from gypsies.

21

Opposition to the Nazis

Who opposed the Nazis? How effective was this opposition?

For much of the 1930s Hitler was very popular, so for many people there was no question of opposing Hitler and the Nazis. Of course all other political parties were banned so it was difficult to organise opposition. The Gestapo dealt ruthlessly with those who did try to oppose Nazi rule. Therefore active opposition to Hitler was always likely to involve a minority of people. Opposition certainly increased during the Second World War. The ever increasing lists of casualties and the food shortages made life in Germany very difficult, but even then most people concentrated on staying alive and finding some food. However, there may have been almost 50 attempts to assassinate Hitler, so someone, somewhere, didn't like him. Who were Hitler's opponents?

A A German reports on life in wartime Germany:

Most people ... are just sticking to the tiring daily business of shopping and thinking about food. The emptiness inside is getting more and more noticeable.

Political opposition

In 1933 all opposition political parties were banned. The main opposition to the Nazis had come from the socialists and the communists. They now were forced to work secretly. However, they were no match for the Gestapo. The two parties did not work together, which made them weaker. As source B suggests, they did not operate secretly enough and so were easily discovered by the Gestapo. Thousands of their members ended up in the concentration camps. Many of them suffered terrible torture.

B Jacob Zorn, a communist, comments on the weakness of the communist opposition:

At first we conducted our resistance relatively openly. We didn't pay proper attention to the rules of conspiracy which you have to follow if you are up against a brutal enemy. I think that is the main reason we suffered such heavy losses.

Opposition from young people

The Edelweiss Pirates

Gangs of young people had developed in the late 1930s (see page 41). There were a number of gangs who regarded themselves as part of a single movement, the Edelweiss Pirates. These included groups such as the 'Travelling Dudes' from Essen, the 'Kittelbach Pirates' from Dusseldorf and the 'Navajos' from Cologne. Initially these groups were largely a protest against the way the Nazis wanted to control every aspect of young people's lives. As the war developed the gangs became more and more involved in organised opposition to the Nazi regime.

C A verse from a Navajo song.

**Hitler's power may lay us low,
And keep us locked in chains,
But we will smash the chains one day,
We'll be free again.
We've got fists and can fight,
We've got knives and we'll get them out,
We want freedom don't we boys?
We're the fighting Navajos.**

Most Pirate groups carried out only small acts of resistance, such as beating up members of the Hitler Youth and writing anti-Nazi slogans on walls. Some went further. For instance, they collected up the propaganda leaflets dropped by allied bombers and pushed them through people's doors. They also offered shelter to deserters from

D The execution of 12 Pirates in Cologne in 1944, following attacks on the Gestapo.

the armed forces. In 1944 the Pirates even attacked the chief of the Gestapo in Cologne. These sort of activities forced the Gestapo to take action. On 7 December the Gestapo arrested 283 gang members in Dusseldorf and another 124 in Essen. In November 12 Pirates were executed in Cologne.

> **E** A part of a White Rose pamphlet from February 1943.
>
> Students! The eyes of the German nation are upon us. Germany expects from us ... the destruction of the National Socialist terror in 1943.

White Rose

The White Rose group were based among students at Munich University. The leaders were Professor Kurt Huber and students Hans and Sophie Scholl. They were arrested by the Gestapo and tortured before being executed. Sophie Scholl had her leg broken during her 'interrogation' and had to limp in agony to the scaffold to be hanged.

The army

Hitler depended on the army to carry out his policies. Opposition in the army was a very serious problem. Unlike most opponents, senior army officers came into contact with Hitler. In 1938 Lt-Col Beck resigned as Chief of Staff of the German armed forces. He did not believe that war over the Sudetenland was justified. Along with his successor, General Halder, he plotted to overthrow Hitler. The plan was that when the German army was ordered to invade the Sudetenland, it should instead capture Hitler. The plan never happened. At Munich the British Prime Minister, Neville Chamberlain, gave the Sudetenland to Germany . There would be no war.

In 1944 a group of army officers attempted to assassinate Hitler. Beck was once more involved. He would become the new President of Germany. The leader of the plot was an army officer, Count von Stauffenberg. On 20 July 1944 he was at a meeting with Hitler and other senior army officers at Hitler's headquarters, the Wolf's Lair. This was sited near Tannenberg, where the Germans had smashed the Russian army in the First World War. The bomb was in Stauffenberg's briefcase. He placed it under the table which all the men were around. Shortly before the bomb went off he left the room. Four people were killed, but Hitler escaped without serious injury. Stauffenberg was executed. Beck shot himself.

Originally an army captain was going to bring the bomb to the Wolf's Lair, strapped to his body. Unaware, the army ordered him back to the front. He had to carry the explosives round with him for a year before he got the chance to throw them in a lake.

F Göring inspects the damage caused by the 1944 bomb at the Wolf's Lair, Hitler's headquarters.

1 a) Look at source B. What reason does it give to explain why the communists were not an effective opposition to the Nazis?
  b) What other reasons can you find?
2 Why were the army likely to be a more effective opposition than young people or political parties?

Extended writing

'There was very little opposition to the Nazis before the war. This proves that almost all Germans supported Hitler's political, social and economic policies.' Explain whether you agree or disagree with this interpretation.

22

Total War and the Fall of the Third Reich

What was the effect of the Second World War on Germany? Did Germany's defeat signal the end of the Third Reich? How did Hitler die?

A Hitler, writing in *Mein Kampf*:

War is the most natural, the most ordinary thing. War is constant; war is everywhere. There is no beginning, there is no conclusion of peace. War is life. All struggle is war.

The home front

At first the war had little effect on people living in Germany. *Blitzkrieg* brought quick victories and little suffering to civilians in the German cities.

There were no food shortages and each victory brought new supplies of raw materials.

This did not last. The RAF launched huge bombing raids on German cities. A single raid on Cologne in 1942 killed 40 000 German civilians. By the end of the war over 3.5 million German civilians had died. The Allies were trying to bomb Germany to destruction. The centres of German cities became ruined shells. The Allies hoped that this would destroy Germany's industrial production. They also hoped that it would destroy the morale of the German people.

B 'The enemy sees your light'. Air raids brought terror to German cities.

C *Bombing raid on Berlin 1943* by Wilhelm Wessel, a German painting showing the damage caused by British and American bombers.

D Jacob Schultz describes the aftermath of a British bombing on the city of Darmstadt in November 1944.

> The hospitals were crammed. All preparations counted for nothing. You could travel without a ticket on the train, bicycle on the pavements. There were no windows in the trains, no schools, no doctors, no post, no telephones. You felt completely cut off from the world. To meet a friend who survived was a wonderful experience ... Many people moaned about their losses, yet others seemed almost relieved by their freedom from possessions.

a) **Coal production (figures in millions of tonnes)**

268   315   318   340   348
1940   1941   1942   1943   1944

b) **Tank production**

2200   5200   9200   17300   22100
1940   1941   1942   1943   1944

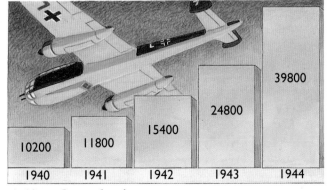

c) **Aircraft production**

10200   11800   15400   24800   39800
1940   1941   1942   1943   1944

E German industrial production (figures adapted from *The Oxford Companion to the Second World War*).

The Germans had to introduce food rationing at the start of the war. At first the German people were allowed much more food than had been the case in the First World War. As the defeats piled up then food became in ever shorter supply and in 1942 food rations were reduced. German civilians were also forced to work much longer hours. A 60-hour week was introduced. There was no full-scale change to a war economy. Unlike the situation in Britain, conscription was not introduced for women. Consumer goods were still produced to try and keep up the morale of civilians. Between 1942 and 1944 Albert Speer, Hitler's architect, was given control of the economy. He closed down small firms and moved workers to bigger and more efficient factories.

In 1941 Hitler launched Operation Barbarossa, the invasion of Russia. Despite early German success, the Russians were able to drive them back. From 1944 onwards cities became full of refugees as people fled from the advancing Red Army in the east.

F The British historian Ian Kershaw on Hitler:

> Hitler's twin obsessions were *Lebensraum* and anti-Semitism. Paranoid hatred of the Jews was the dominant strain, though the two themes fused in Hitler's mind in the vision of Jew-infested Bolshevik Russia, ripe for German expansion.

G A British textbook describes the importance of the war with Russia:

> The invasion of Russia and the destruction of communism had always been Hitler's number one priority. ... It was to become an obsession which cost Germany the war.

1 Why did Britain and America bomb German cities?
2 Do sources D and E suggest that the bombing was successful? Explain your answer.
3 How does source F help to explain why Germany invaded Russia?
4 What does source G suggest was the significance of the war against Russia? What evidence can you find to support this opinion?

THE FALL OF THE THIRD REICH

Hitler had promised that the Third Reich would last for one thousand years. In fact it came to an end after just 12 years.

Hitler stayed in Berlin directing the German war effort from his bunker underneath the Reich Chancellery building. On 22 April the Red Army entered Berlin. On 7 May Germany finally surrendered.

The death of Hitler

It was not Hitler who signed the German surrender. What had happened to him? On 1 May German radio announced that Hitler had died leading his troops against the Red Army. Was this true? Was it merely a cover story to allow Hitler to escape?

A 'The End, the last days of Hitler.' A 1945 Russian painting by Kuprianov, Krilov and Solokov. This is how the Russians imagined the final hours of Hitler's life in the bunker.

B Hugh Trevor-Roper describes Hitler in his final days:

Hitler's eyes, once iceberg blue and shining, were now often glazed, the eyeballs sunken and bloodshot. His brown hair had turned suddenly grey .... In the very last days there was often spittle on his lip, and at times he simply drooled or whistled through his teeth. His complexion was sallow. Soup-slop and mustard spots now stained his once smart and spotless uniform jacket.

After the war a British intelligence officer, Major Hugh Trevor-Roper, was given the task of discovering what had happened to Hitler. In November 1945 he produced his report. He declared that Hitler had shot himself on 30 April. The day before he had married his mistress, Eva Braun. She had committed suicide by taking cyanide. Their bodies had been burnt.

Many people did not believe this conclusion. Trevor-Roper had not been able to interview most of the people who had been with Hitler in the final days. They were either dead or missing. Also Trevor-Roper could not produce any evidence of Hitler's body. There were rumours that all the leading Nazis had managed to escape from Berlin.

C Hitler's will:

My wife and I choose to die in order to escape the shame of overthrow or surrender. It is our wish that our bodies be burnt immediately in the place where I have performed the greater part of my daily work during the course of my twelve years' service to my people.

In 1946 evidence emerged which supported Trevor-Roper's conclusion. An SS officer, Wilhelm Zander, was discovered to be still living in Germany. He had been in Hitler's bunker until 29 April. He had with him three astounding documents. Firstly, the marriage certificate of Hitler and Eva Braun. They had married in the bunker in the early hours of 29 April. She had joined Hitler in the bunker on 15 April, despite being urged by Hitler to flee to safety. Secondly, there was Hitler's will. This stated that he and his new wife intended to commit suicide. Goebbels would be the new Chancellor of Germany. Finally, Goebbels had added his own addition to the will. He would not become the new Chancellor. Instead he would die alongside his *Führer*.

It seemed as though the mystery of Hitler's death had been solved. However, where was the body? The petrol used to burn the body would not have destroyed the bones.

Hitler's body

In 1968 new evidence emerged. The Russians revealed that they had launched an investigation in 1945. Their troops had captured Berlin and entered the bunker. They ought to know what had happened. They revealed that they had found 160 bodies in and around the Chancellery building.

Four of them had been burnt. These were identified as belonging to Hitler and Eva Braun, as well as Goebbels and his wife Magda. Inside the bunker were found the bodies of the Goebbels' six young children. They also found the body of Hitler's double. All had died from cyanide poisoning. So Hitler was dead, but he had not shot himself. An autopsy on his body found splinters of glass from a cyanide capsule in his mouth. This didn't fit with the evidence of those people whom Trevor-Roper had interviewed.

D General Hans Krebs remembers a conversation with Hitler on 29 April. Hitler had asked Krebs' advice on the best way to commit suicide:

'The best way would be to shoot oneself in the mouth.' 'Of course,' Hitler replied, 'but who would finish me off if the wound wasn't mortal?'

E A modern account of 29 April in the bunker, by Ada Petrova and Peter Watson:

Throughout the day of April 29, the mood below ground had been macabre and sombre. It had not been helped by the fact that, during the afternoon, Hitler had had his favourite Alsatian, Blondi, destroyed. The dog had been poisoned by Professor Haase, a former surgeon to the *Führer* as an illustration of what cyanide could do and how quickly it acted.

In August 1991 communist rule in Russia collapsed. The files of the Russian Secret Services gradually came to light. In one was part of a skull which was supposed to be Hitler's. There was also evidence that the Russians had ordered a second investigation in 1946. This had found the skull fragment in the shell crater where Hitler's body had been found the year before. It showed a gunshot wound. The files also revealed that the bodies of the Hitlers and the Goebbels' family had been buried in the grounds of the Smersh (Russian Counter-Intelligence) headquarters in Magdeburg in East Germany. Unfortunately it also revealed that the bodies had been dug up and destroyed in 1970. In that year the Russians had handed over the building to the East Germans. The Russians did not want the bodies accidentally discovered. They might become a shrine for future German worshippers of Hitler. Despite all the terrible evidence, the ideas of Hitler still attract some people today.

F A letter from Magda Goebbels to her son by an earlier marriage, written on 28 April:

God will forgive me as a mother provided I have the courage to carry out this deed and do not leave it to others. When the time comes, I shall give my darlings sleeping potions and then poison.

G Hitler as a toilet brush. Not everyone in Germany remembers Hitler as a hero. This brush was produced in Munich to raise money to help the victims of the Nazis.

Q

1 Look at source A. How does it show life in the bunker?
2 Do you think that source A is likely to be an accurate picture? What evidence can you find which supports this view?
3 What evidence can you find to suggest that Hitler shot himself?
4 What evidence can you find to suggest that Hitler poisoned himself?
5 How do you think that Hitler died? Explain your answer.

Glossary

abdicate – when a monarch gives up the throne

anti-Semitism – the hatred and persecution of the Jews

armistice – an end of fighting in a war

autarky – economic self-sufficiency

censorship – stopping the publication of opposing views

coalition – a government formed by two or more political parties

communist – communists believe in a system of government which opposes democracy and individual freedom and follows government control of the economy

conscription – the compulsory recruitment of men, and sometimes women, into the armed forces

constitution – a set of laws and rules which control how a country is governed

democracy – a system of government where the leaders are voted in to office by the people

hereditary – the right to rule is gained by being closely related to the previous ruler

left-wing – wanting change, especially for the benefit of the working class

nationalised – a nationalised industry is an industry which is controlled by the state or government

pacifist – someone who thinks that war is wrong and should be avoided at all costs

raw materials – these are the materials needed by industry to make their products – for instance iron, coal and oil

reparations – payments made by the defeated countries to repair the damage done to the victorious countries

revolution – the overthrow of a monarchy or government

right-wing – in favour of keeping things the way they are

socialist – socialists believe in a system of government which supports democracy and a greater government involvement in economy and society